Who is Charlie?

For my father

Who is Charlie?

Xenophobia and the New Middle Class

Emmanuel Todd

Maps and diagrams by Philippe Laforgue

Translated by Andrew Brown

polity

First published in French as *Qui est Charlie? Sociologie d'une crise religieuse*, © Éditions du Seuil, 2015
This English edition © Polity Press, 2015, Reprinted 2015, 2016

Polity Press
65 Bridge Street
Cambridge CB2 1UR, UK

Polity Press
350 Main Street
Malden, MA 02148, USA

ISBN-13: 978-1-5095-0577-7

A catalogue record for this book is available from the British Library.

Library of Congress Cataloging-in-Publication Data

Todd, Emmanuel, 1951- author.
    [Qui est Charlie? English]
    Who is Charlie? xenophobia and the new middle class / Emmanuel Todd. -- English edition.
        pages cm
    French edition published: Paris : Seuil, [2015] under title, Qui est Charlie? Sociologie d'une crise religieuse.
    Includes bibliographical references and index.
    ISBN 978-1-5095-0577-7 (Hardback)
    1. Xenophobia--France. 2. Social classes--France. 3. Religion and social status--France. 4. Religion and sociology--France. 5. Social problems--France. 6. Islamaphobia--France. 7. France--Social conditions--1995- I. Title.
    HN440.S62T6313 2015
    306.440944--dc23

                                                            2015022107

Typeset in Adobe Janson on 10.75/14pt by
Servis Filmsetting Limited, Stockport, Cheshire
Printed and bound in the United Kingdom by Clays Ltd, St Ives PLC

The publisher has used its best endeavours to ensure that the URLs for external websites referred to in this book are correct and active at the time of going to press. However, the publisher has no responsibility for the websites and can make no guarantee that a site will remain live or that the content is or will remain appropriate.

For further information on Polity, visit our website:
politybooks.com

Contents

And all must love the human form,
In heathen, Turk, or Jew;
Where Mercy, Love, and Pity dwell
There God is dwelling too.

William Blake, 'The Divine Image', 1789

Preface to the English Edition

In all Western societies, a Charlie lies slumbering. In all of these societies, a dominant social stratum, a middle class reaping the benefits of globalization, and comprising the highly educated and the well-off as well as the elderly, is ready to defend its privileges and, above all, its sense of moral superiority, against the excluded – indigenous workers and the children of immigrants. In all of them, the extending of higher education has dissolved the homogeneous body of citizens, and freedom of trade has led to increasing wage inequality. In all of them, liberal democracy is gradually changing into an oligarchical system that restricts real citizenship to just half the population at most. In all of them, this privileged body of active citizens is anxious, feverish, gnawed by an ever-increasing economic uncertainty, by the vacuum of a culture that has replaced religious values with the values of the stock exchange or a monetary idol. Everywhere, Charlie rules, but he does not know where he is going. Even though he consciously claims to be following positive universal values, he is unconsciously on the look-out for a scapegoat. Everywhere, xenophobia, until recently a characteristic of the poorer sections of society, is starting to pervade the upper half of the social structure, generating a long-term oscillation between Islamophobia and Russophobia.

As a result, in all Western societies, a fit of 'French-style' collective hysteria is possible if a senseless act of terrorism suddenly brings the 'universal' Charlie back to the reality of the unjust and violent world that he dominates and condones.

This book has been written by a Frenchman exasperated by his own society. He has no sympathy for a France that idiotically thinks of itself as the heir to the Great Revolution of 1789, to the values of liberty and equality, to the idea of the universal human being, at the very same time as the behaviour of its ruling classes is in practice unequal and anti-liberal, more reminiscent of the darkest hours in French history, the periods of the Dreyfus Affair and the Vichy Regime. There is no naively idealistic Islamophilia in this book. While it argues in favour of an accommodation with Islam, it also points to the evidence of a real anti-Semitism spreading among many young people of Arab origin in the French suburbs. It takes apart the infernal machinery that leads from a decaying or 'zombie' Catholicism to Islamophobia, and then from a decaying Islam towards anti-Semitism. It also suggests that, if things continue this way, anti-Semitism will return to its source, the middle classes, and in an even more dangerous form. But not just in France. It would be a ridiculous mistake to believe that the author views France as particularly affected by all these regressive developments, and thinks that his own country is particularly despicable or bears a special guilt. France is just a typical example. Things could be more or less serious in other countries, depending on whether their anthropological roots are egalitarian or inegalitarian, and whether their religious past is Catholic or Protestant.

My analysis is based on the anthropology of family structures and the sociology of religions: these make it possible to reach beyond the universality of regressive phenomena to grasp the diversity of Western reactions. A study of what is happening in France is essential, not because this is an extreme case, but because the anthropological and religious duality of France means we can observe differences in behaviour between its central regions (where there is equality on the family level and a deep-rooted attachment to secular values), and its peripheral regions (where inequality and zombie Catholicism are the rule). The diversity of France opens up the possibility of a nuanced approach to the Western world: diverse family structures and values explain the specific temperaments of the Anglo-American, Germanic and Latin worlds. The downward slide of the French system is just one example of the disarray of the Western and, more precisely, the European system. In a final act of modesty, I locate the epicentre of European Islamophobia outside France, as the reader will see: it lies in a world that was once originally Protestant, and more particularly Lutheran, one that has inherited, with dire consequences, the inegalitarian concept of predestination. This claim has not been inspired by any Catholic sense of resentment, as the author's origins are not exactly Catholic.

I was impelled to open my discussion by quoting the last stanza of a poem by William Blake: both for what it has to say about the human and the divine, and also because reading Blake has always given me renewed courage. I insisted on this stanza appearing in English in the original French version of this book, as I wanted to try to remind the French that they are not the only people in the world.

Introduction

We can now say, with the benefit of hindsight, that in January 2015 France succumbed to an attack of hysteria. The massacre of the editorial board of the satirical magazine *Charlie Hebdo*, as well as of several police officers and the customers of a Jewish shop, triggered a collective reaction unprecedented in our country's history. It would have been impossible to discuss it in the heat of the moment. The media joined hands to denounce terrorism, to celebrate the admirable character of the French people, and to sacralize liberty and the French Republic. *Charlie Hebdo* and its caricatures of Muhammad were enshrined. The government announced that it was giving a grant to the weekly so that it could get back on its feet. Crowds of people followed the government's appeal to march in protest throughout the land: they held pencils to symbolize press freedom and applauded the state security police and the marksmen posted on the rooftops. The logo 'Je suis Charlie' ('I am Charlie'), written in white letters against a black background, could be seen everywhere: on our screens, in the streets, on restaurant menus. Children came home from school with a letter C written on their hands. Kids aged seven and eight were interviewed at the school gates and asked for their thoughts on the horror of the events and the importance of one's freedom to draw caricatures. The government decreed that anyone who failed to toe the line would be punished. Any secondary school pupil who refused to observe the minute's silence imposed by the government was seen as implicitly supporting terrorism and refusing to stand in solidarity with the national community. At the end of January, we learned that some adults had started to behave in the most incredibly repressive ways: children of eight or nine years of age were being questioned by the police. It was a sudden glimpse of totalitarianism.

The TV channels and the press told us over and over again that we were living through a 'historic' moment of communion: 'We are one people, France is united in adversity, born anew by and for liberty.' The obsession with Islam was of course ubiquitous. Not only did political journalists listen to imams and ordinary French Muslims telling them, as did everybody else, that violence was unacceptable, that the terrorists were odious and had betrayed their religion. Journalists demanded of these Muslims, as they demanded of all of us, the incantation of the ritual formula 'I am Charlie', which became a synonym for 'I am French'. If they were to be fully accepted as part of the French community, they needed to admit that blasphemy, in the form of caricatures of Muhammad, was an integral element of French identity. It was their *duty* to blaspheme. On our TV screens, journalists wagged a professorial finger as they explained the difference between an act inciting racial hatred (bad), on the one hand, and religious blasphemy (good), on the other. I found it really hard to have to listen to Jamel

Debbouze, a central figure in French culture,[1] being forced to undergo this ordeal when he was interviewed on the TF1 TV channel. He wanted to state that he was a Muslim, that he felt a sense of loyalty to the young people in the suburbs, that he loved France, that he had a non-Muslim wife, that his children had been born from a mixed marriage and that they were the France of tomorrow. He tried to explain to his inquisitor, courteously and painfully, that blasphemy was difficult for a Muslim, that it was not part of his tradition. This was not enough: to be French meant not that you had the *right* to blaspheme, but that it was your *duty*. Thus spake Voltaire. I could not fail to remember what I had read about the Inquisition, which interrogated Jews who had converted to Christianity in an attempt to make sure they really did eat pork, like all true Christians.

The relaunch of *Charlie Hebdo* with a state subsidy marked the zenith of the national reaction to the drama. Its cover yet again allowed us to admire Muhammad, with a face as long as a penis, wearing a turban from which hung two round shapes like testicles. This elegant figure had been drawn on a green background – the colour of Islam – but it was a dull, insipid green, far from the extraordinarily beautiful and subtle greens that adorn Muslim places of worship.[2]

Any historian who studies long-term trends (*la longue durée*) and is familiar with religious crises, when iconophiles and iconoclasts fought it out, cannot fail to observe that when the French state turns an image of Muhammad depicted as a prick into a sacred image, this constitutes a

---

[1] Debbouze is a French/Moroccan actor and comedian. (Translator's note.)

[2] See Claire Courbet, 'Blasphème et sexe en une: l'esprit *Charlie Hebdo* est toujours là!', uploaded on 14 January 2015. The semiologists and media specialists Dominique Wolton and Jean-Didier Urbain analysed the cover of *Charlie Hebdo* for *Le Figaro*.

historic turning-point. France really is going through a religious crisis, one that follows all the religious crises that have given shape to its history, and to European history as a whole, ever since the last days of the Roman Empire. So we can, for once, follow the media in describing the 11 January street demonstrations as 'historic' – a description that was intense, repetitive, obsessive, incantatory; in short: religious.

At that time, I refused to take part in any interviews and debates on the crisis.

And yet I had not hesitated to express my opinion in 2005, when the suburbs erupted into rebellion: I stated that the young people setting cars on fire all over the place were absolutely French. Their acts were strictly speaking criminal, but in my view merely expressed a demand for equality, one of the two fundamental French values. I also emphasized the admirable restraint of the French police, who did not open fire on these kids from the suburbs any more than they had started shooting at the middle-class youngsters in May 1968. In 2005, France was tolerant and free, in spite of the reactions that were naturally and deservedly hostile to the disorder. It was useful to say what one felt. Neither the government, nor journalists, nor society as a whole had succumbed to panic. There was no trace of hysteria to be seen. In 2005, we, the French people, were admirable. We kept our emotions to ourselves. The fear felt by elderly people was silent and led, without any immediate threat to the freedom of expression, to Nicolas Sarkozy's election as president in 2007. The average age of his electorate was higher than for all the right-wing presidents who had preceded him.

But in January 2015, a critical analysis would not have gained a hearing. How could anyone have claimed that this mass mobilization, far from being 'admirable', showed a lack of sang-froid and, in a word, a lack of dignity under pressure? Or that condemning the terrorist act in no way implied that you were divinizing *Charlie Hebdo*? Or that the right to blaspheme *against your own religion* should not be confused with the right to blaspheme *against someone else's religion*, especially in the fraught socioeconomic context of contemporary French society: repetitive and systematic blasphemy against Muhammad, the central character in the religion of a group that is weak and discriminated against, should – whatever the law courts have to say – be treated as an incitement to religious, ethnic or racial hatred.

How could anyone oppose virtuous ignorance on the march, or dare to state that these demonstrators, with their pencils as symbols of liberty, were insulting history, since, in the anti-Semitic and Nazi sequence of events, caricatures of dark-skinned, hook-nosed Jews had led to physical violence? How could anyone explain calmly, taking their time to argue their case, that the most urgent thing for French society in 2015 was not an investigation of Islam but an analysis of how it had become paralysed? How could anyone show that the Kouachi brothers and Amedy Coulibaly were indeed French, the products of French society, and that the use of Islamic symbols does not inevitably turn those who resort to them into real Muslims? Or that these men were merely the mirror image, a pathological reflection, of the moral mediocrity of our elected leaders, more intent on ensuring they get their maximum pension than on freeing young people from the exploitation inherent in the low wages they are paid or the way they are marginalized by unemployment?

How was it possible, in the heat of the moment, to suggest that François Hollande, by deciding to call for a mass demonstration, risked glorifying the Kouachi brothers, conferring an ideological meaning on an act that should have been given its true and lesser worth by a psychiatric-style interpretation? After all, madness, as a loss of contact with reality, needs the ordinary forms of social symbolism: schizophrenics imagine they are Napoleon or Jesus, paranoiacs think they are being penetrated by the sun or persecuted by the state. It would have been possible to view the action of the Kouachi brothers with a certain disdain, thereby weakening its meaning. This kind of approach did not, of course, rule out a sociology of the psychosis of Islamism in France. But such an approach was rejected. Instead, we had the dubious privilege of seeing the authorities endow the problem with a negative sacred aura, and this entailed an aggravation of the religious tensions in our society and in our relations with the rest of the world. This had been Bush's choice in 2001, albeit on the basis of much more serious events. Were the 17 people who died on 7 January really the equivalent of the 2,977 who died in the World Trade Center? Even more than an America so often mocked for its emotional excesses, France overreacted. What had happened on 11 January 2015 to the rational, ironic, witty cast of mind associated with France?

How can people be persuaded to admit that France, as a whole, in its middle classes and not just on its margins, is going through a crisis that is no longer just economic but also religious, or quasi-religious, because the country no longer knows where it is going? The problem of French society cannot be reduced to the suburbs ravaged by the rise of Islamic terrorism: it is much more far-reaching. The focus on Islam actually reveals a pathological need among the middle and upper strata to hate something or someone, and not just the fear of a threat arising from the lower depths of society, even if the number of young jihadists heading off to Syria or Iraq also deserves sociological analysis. Xenophobia used to be confined to the poorer sections of society, but these days it is moving up to the top of the social structure. The middle and upper classes are seeking their scapegoat.

And then there was the disturbing way that the commentaries underplayed the anti-Semitic dimension of the event, even though it came after the killings in Brussels in May 2014 and Toulouse in March 2012. The real question for France is not the right to caricature, but the rise of anti-Semitism in the suburbs. Racism is spreading towards the top and the bottom of the social structure at the same time.

Too many complex, paradoxical, counterintuitive things needed to be explained. It was impossible, in January 2015, to venture such an explanation at a time of national and republican self-celebration. Throughout that period, the state sent its police vans and armed soldiers across France, meticulously positioning them in places where there was absolutely no risk. The new terrorism does not strike blindly; it chooses its targets: blaspheming Islamophobes, police officers, practising Jews. Three guards posted in the right place could probably have prevented the killings at *Charlie Hebdo*, whose offices had long since been labelled a target by Islamic terrorists. The Interior Minister, who had failed in his task, nonetheless strutted around without attracting any criticism. In short, everything about the way the state behaved in January 2015 was rather ridiculous, but anyone who pointed this out would have been seen, given the unanimous atmosphere of the time, as offering support to terrorism.

I also remember that I greeted the news of a lorry drivers' strike as the first signal of a return to reality, a proof that the France everyone envies had survived – the individualistic and egalitarian France that does not take orders from above.

I don't regret having waited. What a researcher can usefully contribute to the public debate is not a purer morality or a better-quality ideology, but an objective interpretation of facts that have escaped the notice of those who actually took part in the events, who were swept away by emotion, impelled by often obscure or downright unconscious emotions. And the 'I am Charlie' of those weeks, whether it expressed the real will of the masses or was a piece of pure media tactics, was, at the heart of our post-industrial society, an emblematic demonstration of false consciousness.

The 11 January demonstrations were interpreted as the re-emergence of a united, resolute France. The Republic reaffirmed its values, with as many images of Marianne as were necessary. Strength, grandeur, rebirth: you could not fail to sense the aspiration to a collective identity, a rise in national feeling, here defining itself as against religious intolerance. The crowds of 11 January were far from being unlikeable, of course. They were marching on behalf of a respect for liberty, with a scattering of flags of every nation, stating loud and clear the difference between radical Islam, which was rejected, and ordinary Islam, accepted just as much as Catholicism if it respected the French principle of secularism. However, the demonstrations did not mention equality. The exclusion of the National Front gave a particular stamp to the event, which was now 'guaranteed 100 per cent non-xenophobic'. The demonstrations were peaceful and well behaved. Also, it was difficult to get those taking part to provide any precise justifications for their presence in the crowd. The main feeling was the need to 'stand together' after the horror, to affirm a few basic 'values'.

So it would be wrong to imagine that the crowds of 11 January were essentially like-minded in the same way that the unanimous media were. Hard-line secularists of the kind who gobble down priests, rabbis and imams for breakfast marched alongside the many more numerous people who justified their presence as showing a general support for freedom of expression and the need to defend an ideal of tolerance. Several discussions convinced me that, in the days after the 'republican march', tens of thousands of participants definitely, and perhaps even hundreds of thousands, wondered what they had really done, or condoned, by joining the march on that day. Many of them experienced the 'I am Charlie' event as an episode in which they were alienated in and by the thoughts of others, suffered a temporary depersonalization and ended up with an ideological hangover that shortly led to the memory of the whole thing being consigned to the file labelled 'Very Bad Trips'.

But we are still only at the conscious, explicit level here. We need to dig deeper and inquire into the sociological factors that led these crowds to gather in a state of spiritual communion.

There was a part of France that was not there on 11 January, and the part that *was* there, anxious to pass itself off as the whole, was neither as sure of its values nor as generous of spirit. The poorer sectors of the population were not Charlie; the young people from the suburbs, whether Muslim or not, were not Charlie; the provincial working classes were not Charlie. On the other hand, the France of the upper-middle classes was out in superior force, as it were, and on that day it showed that it was able to take the middle strata of French society along with it thanks to the way it could express its emotions. And yet even today the French middle classes, far from being the bearers of the 'positive values of the nation', are fundamentally selfish, autistic and repressive in mood. They have even abandoned the principle of equality. And they are often, as we shall see, closer to the old Catholic bedrock of France than to the tradition of secularism. In short, they may be the France of today, but they are definitely not the France of the revolutionary tradition.

At this point, the Marxist concept of false consciousness and the Freudian notion of the unconscious spring to mind. In particular, we need to return to Émile Durkheim's definition of sociology: this discipline, he says, starts to be a science when it accepts that human beings are sometimes driven by social forces that transcend them. Their conscious interpretation of their actions is not always correct. This is why the founding text of modern sociology, Durkheim's *Suicide*, begins by rejecting the explanations that some people who commit suicide leave behind them and the reasons given by the officials who register their deaths. Instead, Durkheim seeks the meaning, or rather meanings, of this phenomenon in the objective statistical distribution of acts of suicide – in time, in space, and according to family situation and religion. This is exactly what we need to do if we are to grasp the 'I am Charlie' phenomenon. This approach means we will leave out the demonstrators who were often unable to give any real explanation for what they were doing there, and we will ignore the political journalists who assumed the task of giving us 'the meaning behind it all', and were swept away by the copycat intoxication of an overcrowded media field.

We must not go too far in absolving people because they were unconscious of what was driving them, however. We have also had to deal with cowardice and cynicism. The politicians consciously exploited the event to try to escape from their unpopularity, and many journalists deliberately neglected their critical duties. As for the crowds, which were admittedly made up of many different elements, uncertain and likeable as they were, we cannot absolve them straightaway just because they were not conscious of their motives. Ignorance of the law is no excuse; there is no excuse for not knowing why you are demonstrating. France is lying to itself. Often, France thinks that it is great when it is in fact petty, but sometimes it says it is great when it knows that it is petty. This book is also an essay on lying. Charlie – an impostor?

Who, socially speaking, were the demonstrators? Where did they come from? Answering these two simple questions will enable us to identify the France that took to the streets on 11 January and to recognize in it an old enemy, one that is becoming radicalized and in its own way fundamentalist.

So the time has come to take the events of January 2015 seriously – but we will do this by focusing not on the massacre of Wednesday 7 January, but the exaggerated reaction of French society. The main demonstrations, on Sunday 11 January, gave rise to hasty estimates of the numbers attending: these were probably exaggerated and not always compatible, but they can at least be treated statistically. Between 3 and 4 million demonstrators means between 4.5 and 6 per cent of the French population. The presence of children at these marches debars us from taking these overall figures as representing adults alone. But they can legitimately be seen as including citizens from the 85 biggest urban areas, which gives a very high rate of participation, between 7 and 10 per cent. The demonstrations (taken in their collective sense, including Paris and the provinces) thus spontaneously established themselves, so to speak, as an object for sociological study. So a cartography of these demonstrations will show us what exactly they were.

I have on three occasions carried out a cartographical analysis of French society, in 1981, 1988 and 2011, and when I looked at the map published in *Libération* on 12 January, I immediately felt that the distribution of emotion across French territory was not uniform and that the appropriate statistical treatment could tell us what social and religious, or crypto-religious, forces had brought so many people out onto the streets. Is it not absolutely dumbfounding that estimates rushed out the day after the demonstrations could produce correlations that are, from the point of view of statistical theory, highly significant? Irrespective of this, the unanimity so loudly trumpeted by the media is a fiction. This should not come as a disappointment, and we ought not to draw the conclusion that it was an illusion that has left nothing in its wake. Quite the contrary. Understanding how part of society was able to impose a false image of reality on the population as a whole is to lay bare the reality of our social system. Thus it is that the demonstrations of 11 January, that moment of collective hysteria, present us with a fantastic tool for understanding the mechanisms of ideological and political power in current French society.

Several major surprises await us. For example, we shall see that the present debate on secularism has deviated from the tradition of secular values, and that forces that are now claiming to support the Republic are not in their essence republican: in short, Marianne is no longer the lovable woman we used to know. We will be seeing how the great French political system has seized up at its very heart; we will understand why the Socialist Party has put down anchor on the political right, and why the right is floating around in French waters without really knowing what it is. We shall seek to identify the powerful, efficacious and altogether despicable forces which have confined France to a straitjacket of political and economic policies that are destroying some of its population. We will have to admit that France is no longer France, but we will also have to wonder whether it has any chance of becoming itself again with – why not? – the help, one day in the distant future, of Islam and the electors of the National Front.

But before we start to think up possible remedies, we need to diagnose the illness that has caused the frets and fevers that afflict us. We need to know what kind of society could have brought between three and four million people out onto the streets to show their solidarity with a magazine identified with a caricature of Muhammad, one that specialized in stigmatizing a minority religion, Islam, and designating it as France's number one problem.

The tone of this essay, which was written in a fit of exasperation, is not academic. And yet, for me, it was a question of carrying out a sociology of the event while it was still hot off the press, observing scientific rigour as much as possible while having to work fast, drawing on and deploying, in a few weeks, 40 years' worth of laboriously accumulated research and knowledge. But thanks to the highly original surveys of populations of Catholic and Muslim origin carried out by IFOP, the French national market research institute, and communicated to me by Jérôme Fourquet, the study is up to date and precise. Thanks to the statistical treatment of street demonstrations carried out by Philippe Laforgue, it is rigorous in its methods.

Insofar as this book investigates, simultaneously, the religious foundations and economic structures of society, without seeking too much to establish a hierarchy between them, it closely follows the work of Max Weber. Admittedly, by taking account of family structures, I have rooted my whole approach in something deeper than the variables that Weber focused on. But, as will be seen, I have not viewed the family as a more important factor than religion in assessing the degree of 'egalitarianism' characterizing the regional societies that constitute France as a whole.

This essay follows in the footsteps of Max Weber in an even deeper and more moral sense. As Weber explains in 'Science as a Vocation', sociology should not claim to distinguish between good and evil, but should help human beings to understand the deep sense of their choices and their actions, and force them to acknowledge that it is latent values which lead them to make a particular ideological or political choice. In this way, via analysis and argument, I shall be led, at the end of my discussion, to put forward a certain number of surprising and rather unpleasant propositions on the way the educated masses, the elderly, French people from the Catholic tradition, and Socialists and their leaders all behaved. But in all this I will have tried simply to be faithful to the spirit of Weber: 'Scientists can – and must – tell you that this or that decision you come to derives logically ... from this or that ultimate and fundamental vision of the world ... . Science will point out that, by adopting such a position, you will be serving one god and offending another.'[1]

---

[1] Weber, 'Science as a vocation' (*Wissenschaft als Beruf*), a lecture given in 1917. Emmanuel Todd quotes from the French translation of Weber's work, under the title *Le Savant et le politique*, translated by Lucien Freund (Paris: UGE, 10/18, 1963): this differs considerably from the standard English translation, so I have simply transposed the French version. (Translator's note.)

A Religious Crisis

In their size and the metaphysical claims they were making, the 11 January demonstrations were a clear indication that France was going through a religious crisis. To judge from the disquiet of the demonstrators, the commentators and the government, you would have thought that 15–25 per cent of Muslims were preparing to force their faith onto the country of Joan of Arc, Voltaire and Charles de Gaulle.

Indeed, this was the theme of Michel Houellebecq's latest novel, *Soumission* (*Submission*): it was destined to be a best-seller even before its publication, and before the horrors perpetrated by the Kouachi brothers and Amedy Coulibaly. Éric Zemmour's latest Islamophobic rant had also picked up a huge audience just before the attack happened. His *Le Suicide français* (*French Suicide*) sang the same old tune about the way that integration had failed, multiculturalism was a dead end, and our wonderful culture was at death's door. On 30 October 2014, long before the events of 9 January, Zemmour told the *Corriere della Sera* (Italian daily newspaper) that

France ought to start thinking about sending Muslims home. This eventually triggered a fascinating polemic concerning the semantic condensation in the word 'deportation' used by the Italian interviewer to describe what Zemmour had said. Was this term appropriate or not to describe the expulsion, on board ship, of a sector of the French population?

Islamophobia has its own rhythm. Insofar as it symbolically casts Muslims out of the national community, it is both a cause and an effect of terrorism. It is one of the two poles of an infernal dialectic in which the objective crisis afflicting the French suburbs, and the hysteria of ideology, feed into each other.

However, here as elsewhere, we need to situate the phenomenon sociologically and statistically. Support for Islamophobia, of a Houellebecquo-Zemmourian kind, is essentially confined to those who have the means to buy books and the time to read them – in other words, people of a certain age who belong to the middle classes. Neither the working-class milieus who vote for the National Front, nor young college graduates whose income is falling, have the means or the time to read Zemmour's actual words, or Houellebecq's.

Rather than charging at the red (or rather green) rag of Islam, we should dwell on the spiritual consternation afflicting the 94 per cent of the population that comes from a Christian background. We will be coming back later to the psychological and social state of the 4.5–5 per cent of Muslims who contribute to the existence of the French nation.

We need to treat these disproportionate figures – 94 per cent of Christian origin, 4.5–5 per cent of Muslim origin – with some caution. For each religious affiliation, this assessment includes, along with believers and practising members of their faith, those for whom religion is a memory rather than a present reality. The truth about religion in France in 2015 is that there is a lack of belief on a scale unprecedented in history. Among the totally secularized French we find the majority of children born into mixed marriages, i.e. to married couples from different religious backgrounds: these mixed marriages have sometimes been taking place over several generations. Their ancestry is a fraternal mixture of Christian, Muslim and Jewish elements, not forgetting the Buddhism, Confucianism and Hinduism of our compatriots of Asian origin.

We need to seek our country's religious dynamics in the central mass of French society, of course, and not on its fringes. This methodological decision will help us to remember that, not so long ago, there were crowds out in the streets marching against 'Marriage for all'. On 13 January 2013, two years before Charlie made its dramatic entrance onto the national stage, the most successful of the 'Demos for all' had brought together between 340,000 and 800,000 people in Paris, depending on whether we go with the figures provided by the police or the demonstrators themselves. A significant, often Catholic minority refused to allow that homosexual couples could legally marry. This led to a certain feverishness of a religious or quasi-religious kind in the central mass of French society, in a negative mode, as it were, as the reality of what was actually happening – marriage for all – marked yet one more stage in the nation's continuing break with the traditional Christian vision of the family.

How did this religious crisis reveal itself on 11 January?

The terminal crisis in Catholicism

In France, religion and habits develop in concert. Religious practice finally collapsed, to all intents and purposes, between

1960 and 1990. In 1950, the average woman had three children: this fertility rate has since fallen to two, a change that
includes the disappearance of big Catholic families. In 1960,
5.5 per cent of children were born out of wedlock: these
days, it is 55 per cent. France, where the Church still played
a massive part a few decades ago, is now, in its beliefs and its
habits, a country of sceptics.

Thirty or forty years do not amount to much in the
history of mentalities. Even today, the population pyramid
still bears the imprint of an elderly population with some
attachment to religion, looking down on the younger generations who are completely detached from religion. A recent
IFOP survey gave a figure of 12.7 per cent of those polled
who defined themselves as 'practising' Catholics. If strict
criteria of religious sociology, i.e. counting the number of
people who actually attend mass on Sundays, were applied,
this proportion would probably be halved. The fact remains
that, if the figures obtained from the self-definition of those
polled are just 6.6 per cent for those aged 25–34, it is still
21.6 per cent for the 65–74 age group and 32.7 per cent
for those aged 75 and more.[1] People who are now between
75 and 85 were between 20 and 30 in 1960. Since then, for
this age group, religious practice has thus shrunk to a fifth.[2]
That one-in-three of the 'over-75s' declare themselves to be
practising does not show that France was, around 1960, uniformly Catholic, but already two-thirds de-Christianized.

And yet a fall in the numbers of practising Catholics from
33 per cent to 6 per cent is far from negligible, especially

[1] Jérôme Fourquet and Hervé Le Bras, 'La religion dévoilée. Nouvelle
géographie du catholicisme', Fondation Jean-Jaurès, April 2014, p. 88.
[2] For the purposes of this comparison, I am not considering the possibility of a cycle within each generation that might lead to belief rising again
as one gets older. I doubt that the residual beliefs of the young people of
today will become stronger at the end of their lives.

if it is accompanied by metaphysical disruption among the two-thirds of the population that, in 1960, had long since escaped the grip of Catholicism. France has slipped into a generalized lack of belief and a relaxation of morals, and this leads to problems of psychological and political balance for a population that is constantly changing.

Religious decline and the rise of xenophobia

A comparative study of times of dramatic religious decline in history forces us to raise the question of the psychological problems that such a transition may cause. A transformation or decline in belief is most often followed by some revolutionary event. The disappearance of its metaphysical framework almost automatically leads, in a population, to the emergence of a replacement ideology, whose values may vary but which is most often physically violent.

In France, around 1730–40, the number of priests being recruited in the Paris Basin and on the Mediterranean seafront had dried up, but was being maintained at a normal level in the rest of the kingdom. The French Revolution would follow on from this crisis in Catholicism, half a century later. The Church had guaranteed equality and fraternity to its faithful in their quest for eternal life, thanks to baptism for all and salvation through good works. In 1789, this distant goal was converted into the demand for an immediate liberty and equality in the Earthly City.

Note that Voltaire's *Philosophical Dictionary*, in which he expressed a completely anti-religious set of ideas, combative and droll, was published in 1764, i.e. twenty years *after* the collapse of the Church in two-thirds of the kingdom.

In Germany, between 1880 and 1930, the decline in religious practice in the two-thirds of the country that was

Protestant led to the rise, first, of social democracy and anti-Semitism, and, second, of Nazism. Both Nietzsche's rapturous utterances on the death of God and Weber's religious sociology were also products of this metaphysical crisis. The ideological values that gained a voice in Nazi Germany were the opposite, term by term, of the values of revolutionary France, just as Protestantism had been the metaphysical opposite of the Catholicism of the Paris Basin around 1700. Lutheran predestination stated that human beings had an unequal chance of being saved: they were chosen or rejected even before they were born, by a decree of the Almighty that brooked no appeal. This authoritarian, inegalitarian theology was replaced, in 1933, by the demand for an immediate servitude on earth. Each race chose which people it would accept: the status of human beings was reserved for Aryans, while the Jews were condemned to the hell of the death camps – a secular transposition of the eternal damnation put forward by Luther.

We need to take religion seriously, especially when it starts to disappear. This is not the same as ignoring economic structures and crises: the French Revolution really was triggered by a rise in the cost of wheat, and the Nazi revolution by a wide-scale economic depression. But we also need to admit that neither famine nor unemployment by themselves would have produced such massive and intense (and victorious) revolutionary phenomena. The violence that attended their beginnings means that the French Revolution and Nazism attained in their own time – and still preserve in our memories – what might be called a 'metaphysical status'. These events both emerged from a religious crisis, and were themselves in one sense religious.

Earthly ideologies differ in content because deep family values, latent anthropological systems, continue to guide the choices made by societies when they escape from the grip of religion in the strict sense of the term. In the heart of the Paris Basin, a liberal and egalitarian family structure regulated social behaviour; in Germany, an authoritarian and inegalitarian family structure gave it a completely different hue.

We are experiencing economic problems that are less brutal but longer lasting than the Great Crash of 1929. However, the political future of our society depends on a religious or quasi-religious transformation taking place beneath the surface every bit as much as it depends on obvious economic developments.

The terminal crisis of Catholicism affected the Western world as a whole from the 1960s onwards. Where this was the religion of populations that were linguistically in a minority or felt they were under cultural domination – in Quebec, the Basque Country, Ireland and Flanders – its disappearance led, from the 1970s, to a strong rise in nationalism. The shift to secularism produced an upsurge of terrorism in Canada, Spain and Ireland, and less violent – but perhaps longer-lasting – attacks of xenophobia in Belgium. The Flemish still show a remarkable hatred for French-speaking territories, even though these same Flemish have become the domi-nant group in their own country. All these events occurred in a period of prosperity and development in the respective consumer societies.

It is important to understand the logic that can lead from Catholicism to xenophobia. The Catholic Church, attached as it is to the principle of hierarchy, is nonetheless univer-sal by tradition, as its name suggests. Until around 1960, the Church acted as a moderating influence in certain regional cultures that were not inclined to universalism: more precisely, it actively kept ethnocentrism in check. Québécois, Basque, Irish and Flemish cultures were like German culture in that they lacked the principle of family equality. So Catholicism incorporated the ethnocentrism of its anthropological base into a system that may have been authoritarian and vertical but still had a universal vocation. It was only logical that the disappearance of this regulator should have liberated the inegalitarian or non-egalitarian temperament rooted in family structures that ran even deeper than Catholicism.

From the second half of the 1980s, the decline of Catholicism led to analogous effects in Italy, where the Lega Nord turned its in-house xenophobia against southerners, those from the *Mezzogiorno*. Its regional epicentre, northeast of the Po, corresponds closely to the regions of Italy where religious practice was, until around 1960, at its strongest, and where the anthropological base did not predispose people to universal values.

In Poland and western Ukraine, communist oppression had kept a defensive Catholicism alive and well. In the case of western Ukraine, this was, more precisely, the Uniate religion, i.e. one that had originally been Orthodox but had joined with Catholicism during the seventeenth century. As the sharp fall in fertility statistics after 1990 shows, this self-protective version of Catholicism did not survive the fall of communism. Its disappearance left a vacuum, which traditionally entails anxiety and a rise in xenophobia, independent of the material context, since Poland adapted well to the new economic conditions, while Ukraine failed completely. In the context of post-communist Eastern Europe, the replacement of one system by another could lead only to a rise in Russophobia, just as analogous phenomena had previously entailed Anglophobia, Hispanophobia, Francophobia and Italophobia in Western Europe, depending on the place.

It is plausible that a similar process played a role in the secession of Croatia, a country defined by its Catholicism. However, I would hesitate to place it in the same category as Poland or western Ukraine, since the civil war that destroyed Yugoslavia, even though this country was defined by Catholic, Orthodox and Muslim religious identities, was triggered by the collapse of communism rather than by the decline of the Church.

The emergence of a far right tinged with neo-Nazi elements in the Ukrainian provinces of Galicia, Volhynia and Ruthenia comes as a surprise to people who imagine that populations that have been liberated must be psychologically more balanced. But those who had been forewarned by their observation of the emergence of Basque, Irish, Flemish and Québécois nationalism thought it was only to be expected. This should help us understand that while Russophobia in Poland and western Ukraine resorts to a set of symbols from the past, it expresses a religious crisis that is being experienced in the present, one that has little to do with Russia's will to power.

The way nationalism chooses its goals and the objects of its hatred rarely shows much originality. However, we are forced to admit that the terminal crisis of Catholicism in France and Germany has produced a much more interesting ideological form of transition than any mere ethnocentric nationalism. We need to point out that in both countries the practising Catholic provinces comprised only a third of the territory, and had been fully integrated into their respective nations by the First World War. But the decline of Catholicism contributed greatly, on both sides of the Rhine, to the rise in pro-European sentiment that led to the Treaty of Maastricht. In the case of France, this is demonstrated by political cartography.

The decay of Catholicism in France, combined with the egalitarian and universalist heritage at the heart of the national system, has led to an anxiety which in turn has fostered the emergence of a hybrid but grandiose ideological form, an attempt to create a multinational nationalism.

Catholic France and secular France: 1750–1960

There is not, after all, just one Catholic France but two: first, a Catholic France that abandoned the Church in the middle of the eighteenth century, and second, a Catholic France that stayed faithful to it until around 1960 but has finally kicked free and lost its belief. So there are now two de-Christianized Frances in our country, the one old, the other very recent, its territory defined by Map 1.1a.

Thanks to the work of Timothy Tackett, we know that it was not individuals who left Catholicism in the eighteenth century, but certain local communities, while other local communities stayed faithful to the Church.[1]

The Civil Constitution of the Clergy in 1791 wanted priests and bishops to be elected by their parishioners. Priests were required to swear allegiance to this measure. Map 1.1b, based on Tackett's data, shows how many agreed to swear and how many refused. But far from giving us any insight into the priests' real thoughts, this shows us what the parishes wanted. Priests accepted the constitution in a huge swathe of the Paris Basin, from Saint-Quentin to Bordeaux, as well as on the Mediterranean seafront, itself linked to Paris via a corridor including the *départements* of the Drôme, Isère, Ain and Saône-et-Loire. They rejected the republican Church in a constellation of peripheral provinces: the west as a whole, most of the southwest and the Massif Central, the Jura, Alsace and the northernmost regions.

From 1793 onwards, the Revolution aimed to confront and destroy the Church. It failed, thereby perpetuating the first fracture in the religious space of France.

---

[1] Timothy Tackett, *Religion, Revolution, and Regional Culture in Eighteenth-Century France: The Ecclesiastical Oath of 1791* (Princeton, NJ: Princeton University Press, 1986).

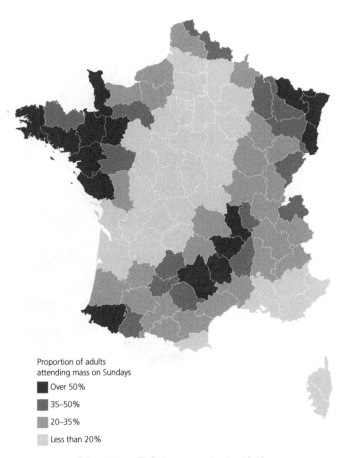

Proportion of adults
attending mass on Sundays

■ Over 50%

■ 35–50%

■ 20–35%

□ Less than 20%

Map 1.1a   Religious practice in 1960

Religious choices are far from an individual matter, so the geography of mentalities had hardly altered when, in the wake of the Second World War, the church canon Boulard and Gabriel Le Bras drew up the first national map of religious practice (Map 1.1a).[1] The de-Christianized

[1] The final results of this research can be found in *L'Atlas de la pratique religieuse des catholiques en France* by François André Isambert and Alain Terrenoire (Paris: Presses de la Fondation des sciences politiques, 1980).

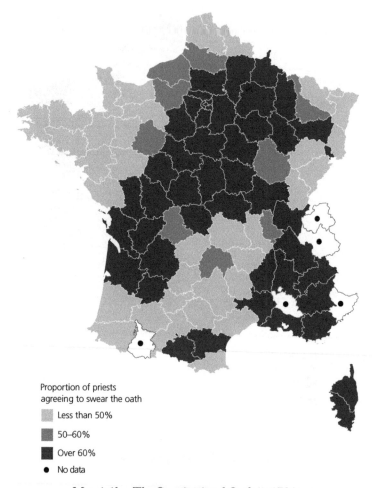

Map 1.1b   The Constitutional Oath in 1791

Proportion of priests
agreeing to swear the oath

Less than 50%

50–60%

Over 60%

● No data

heart of France appears to be stable, with two poles, still
including as it does the Paris Basin and the Mediterranean
seafront. The Catholic constellation round the periphery is almost intact. The front lines have hardly changed.
The Limoges region, the valley of the Garonne and the
Nord-Pas-de-Calais are drifting away from the Church;

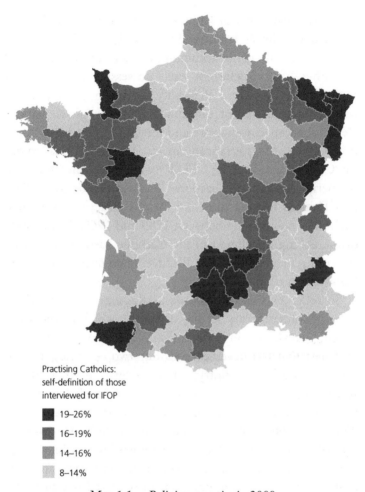

Practising Catholics:
self-definition of those
interviewed for IFOP

■ 19–26%

■ 16–19%

■ 14–16%

□ 8–14%

Map 1.1c   Religious practice in 2009

the Rhône-Alpes region, Lorraine and Cotentin seem to be returning to it.

This stability is evidence of the 'futility' of the religious struggle that was waged for over a century – from the 200,000 dead in the Vendée wars between 1793 and 1796, to the harsh stocktaking of the clergy's assets during the separation between Church and State in 1905. Indeed, the struggle simply confirmed the coexistence in France of two separate religious communities, one of believers and the other of non-believers, each possessing its own territory. Under the Third Republic, the interplay of political parties became part of this fundamental religious pattern. Republicanism, communism and the CGT[1] flourished in the central and Mediterranean areas. The traditional right, the CFCT[2] and later the CFDT,[3] were established forces in the peripheral Catholic bastions. The contrast between these two Frances formed the fundamental structure of French social and political life between 1789 and 1960. And in spite of the ebbing of religion in the Catholic bastions, this division of French territory is still active, in an unconscious way, below the surface.

So religious sociology shows us the anti-historical character of contemporary secular discourse, which is frenziedly pitted against 'communitarianism'. It refers, as it were, to a past that has never existed. For two centuries, France was a Janus-faced country, simultaneously mother of the Revolution and eldest daughter of the Church, communitarian in practice at the local level. The true genius of the Third Republic will have resided in its ability to maintain a Jacobin discourse of Unity and Indivisibility, while at the same time practising a pragmatic communitarianism – or, more precisely, a communitarianism rendered pragmatic by a century and a half of conflicts between the Republic and

[1] Confédération générale du travail, a group of French trade unions, traditionally on the left. (Translator's note.)
[2] Confédération française des travailleurs chrétiens, a group of French trade unions, social Christian in orientation. (Translator's note.)
[3] Confédération française démocratique du travail, the branch of the CFCT that split off to become a secular confederation of trade unions. (Translator's note.)

the Church. In the end, Marianne got used to cohabiting with the Virgin Mary.

In actual fact, French secularism did not consist in an aggregate of private consciences deciding whether or not to believe in God. On national territory, it combined a culture of unbelief with vast numbers of those in peripheral regions who had remained Catholic. Over time, a *modus vivendi* was established on the national scale. Individuals and families, in moderate proportions, took advantage of this balance to live their Catholic beliefs in peace (in the de-Christianized zone), or to enjoy their unbelief (in the Catholic zone). Religious minorities – Jews emancipated in 1791 and Protestants who had survived the Revocation of the Edict of Nantes in 1685 – sided politically with the unbelievers. This was a sensible decision to take, but it did quickly lead them to adopt an elegant religious scepticism.

The two Frances and equality

What lies behind this enduring division within France? There was one word that was not much heard during the crisis of January 2015: the word 'equality'. Charlie was content just to affirm his liberty. And yet it is the second term in the motto of the French Republic that helps us most easily understand the contrast between the two Frances. Long before the fracturing of the national territory by the first crisis in Catholicism, what we find, with regard to the relationship with equality, is a division between centre and periphery, a contrast that has been defined, ever since the end of the Middle Ages, by family structures.

Traditional peasant family structures in the heart of the Paris Basin and on the Mediterranean seafront were egalitarian, especially in the part of Provence closest to the sea.

In the north of the country, egalitarianism included girls, since they had the right to an equal share in inheritance with their brothers. In the south, a patrilineal bias favoured boys. So the heart of the national system, with its annex on the Mediterranean, spontaneously believed in equality. An unconscious mechanism was at work: 'If brothers are equal, then men are equal and peoples are equal.' We here find the source of the revolutionary concepts of civic equality and the universality of mankind. Mass literacy in the eighteenth century ensured the ideological crystallization of these ideas.

On the other hand, the family structures of peripheral France were, in their various different ways, not egalitarian. There was an overt preference for inequality only in those countries that practised the right of primogeniture, with a huge southwest area pushing a tentacle out towards the Alpes-Rhône region, as well as in some parts of coastal Brittany, and in Alsace.[1] In the west as a whole and the Nord-Pas-de-Calais the dominant family systems were not altogether inegalitarian, but nor were they, as those in the Paris Basin were, obsessed with the division of inheritances into equal parts.

The two Frances have long formed a systematic ensemble. Without the counterweight of peripheral France, which fosters discipline, the egalitarian individualism of the heart of the national system would have produced disorder rather than a doctrine of liberty and equality. From the point of view of the anthropology of family structures, the real France, in the long term, might well consist of two-thirds anarchy and one-third hierarchy.

---

[1] The formal egalitarianism of Alsace was, as throughout the Rhineland, inactive in actual practice.

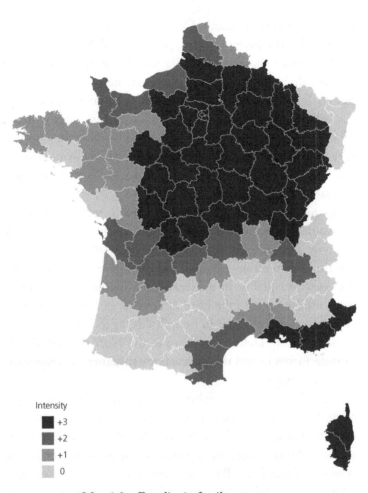

Map 1.2   Equality in family structures

Map 1.2 gives a simplified vision of the original division of
the principle of family equality in France. It defines the basic
anthropology of the nation. However, it ignores the intermediate forms that, since the end of the Middle Ages, have
welded the central block to its periphery, particularly the *oil*

part of France to its south, Occitania,[1] along an axis running through La Rochelle, Poitiers, Bourges and Nevers.

More often than not, equality in the family was linked to liberal values. At the heart of the Paris Basin, children from the nuclear peasant family quickly became emancipated. But the communitarian family of the northwest edges of the Massif Central, between Dordogne and the Nièvre, although very egalitarian, was not liberal: here, the individual often lived in the context of extended households that included several married couples.

Inequality was frequently associated with authoritarian values. The stem family of the southwest and Alsace brought generations together in vertical structures covering three generations, combining the father's authority and the sons' inequality in a hierarchical totality. In the inner west, indifference to the ideal of equality could be combined with a nuclear structure in households, as in England. In the Vendée, in the Deux-Sèvres and in the Nord-Pas-de-Calais, flexible forms linked the generations together in temporary, pragmatic ways.

But it is the map of equality that explains not just the origin of de-Christianization, but also the emergence of those bastions that resisted such a process. The ebb of Catholic belief in the eighteenth century began in the heart of the egalitarian systems of the Paris Basin and the Mediterranean seafront. The fundamental formula of 'egalitarian' de-Christianization is simple: once they had learned to read and write, the populaces rejected the hypothesis of a God superior to human beings and a priest superior to his parishioners. Conversely,

---

[1] In the Middle Ages, '*oil*' was 'yes' in the form of French spoken in the north of the country; 'oc' was the equivalent word in the south, hence 'Occitania'. (Translator's note.)

in the bastions of Catholicism, no egalitarian family was unconscious of the threat of religion's authority.

The maps of family equality and de-Christianization coincide only imperfectly. Only the identity of the poles is evident. It is clear that de-Christianization, at first structurally defined by the egalitarianism of family structures, then spread along the main arteries of communication. We can see it penetrate the southwest down the Paris/Bordeaux axis, along the line of the future *autoroute* A10, before moving up along the valley of the Garonne.

In the context of this essay, devoted as it is to the current crisis in French society, and thus to the country's future rather than its origins, it is not necessary to go into the parallels and divergences between the egalitarianism of family structures and de-Christianization in any great detail. If we are to understand what is happening, it will be more useful to define a synthetic map of the egalitarian temperament in the territory of France, adding together and, as it were, superimposing the egalitarianism of the family structure and that of the 'de-Christianized' mentality. If the family defines brothers as equal, and if religious scepticism says that ordinary human beings do not need to submit to priests or to God, the level of latent egalitarianism in a local culture will reach a maximum. If the family is inegalitarian and lives in a Catholic milieu, the level of latent egalitarianism will be at a minimum. Discordant combinations give intermediate scores.

I have therefore added family egalitarianism and irreligion together on Map 1.3 to obtain an overall score for equality from 0 to 3. The existence of huge intermediate spaces suggests that there is a tension between the principles of equality and inequality, ebbs and flows in the territory of France. Until the early 1980s, maps of voting patterns in France mainly revealed the importance of the Catholic stamp. The retreat of

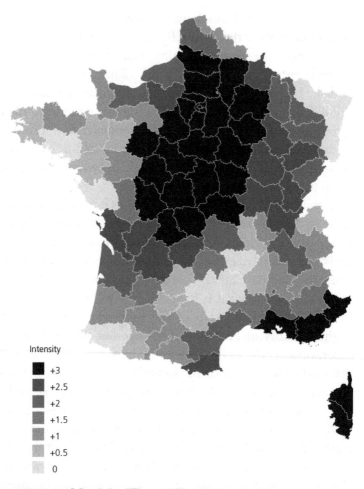

Intensity

- ■ +3
- ■ +2.5
- ■ +2
- ■ +1.5
- ■ +1
- ■ +0.5
- ■ 0

Map 1.3   The overall egalitarian backdrop

the Church leads gradually to a rise in latent family egalitarianism, or in its opposite, in the way people vote. Until around 1990, the map of religious practice was most effective when it came to predicting the stable political alignment of the different regions; in 2015, the map which combines family structure and religion seems the most appropriate. I will systematically be using these 'equality scores' in Chapter 4 to explain the meaning of votes cast in 2012 for Marine Le Pen, Nicolas Sarkozy, François Hollande and Jean-Luc Mélenchon.

From the One God to the single currency

Just over twenty years ago, the Maastricht Treaty led to the greater part of Western Europe indulging in the dream of a unification via its currency. This was approved by a referendum in France in 1992, with 51 per cent of the vote, after intense debate. Today the plan appears to have been crazy: the Eurozone, in spite of every budgetary, financial and, above all, ideological effort, is a festering mass of stagnation, unemployment and deflation. Now that we have been liberated of the need to debate the project's economic advantages, we can calmly and dispassionately examine the anthropological and religious origins of this utopian scheme.

The electorate's approval of Maastricht brought out a vertical dimension of position in the class structure and a horizontal dimension of geographical location on the centre/periphery axis.

The referendum first and foremost highlighted the notion of social class. It brought to national awareness – one might even say it gave birth to – the now permanent theme of an opposition between the elites and the people. At the top of the social structure, 70 per cent of 'executives and superior intellectual [i.e. liberal] professions' voted 'yes', and in their wake 57 per cent of the 'intermediary professions' were also positive. At the bottom, the poorer classes were spontaneously hostile to the treaty. Only 42 per cent of workers approved, and 44 per cent of employees; the figure was the same for artisans and small shopkeepers.

The socio-professional categories used by INSEE, the

French National Institute for Statistics and Economic Research, combine the economic and cultural dimensions of a person's social status. Above all, we should not jump to the conclusion that managerial and liberal professions are necessarily well-paid. This group includes university and secondary school teachers as well as the other civil servants in cadre A of the civil service, a world with its own consistency but one where salaries are nothing special. So the so-called 'superior' group involves both educational advantages and economic advantages, in income and/or job security. Primary school teachers and educational advisors all fall into the 'intermediate' professions, which, politically speaking, voted the same way as those in the 'superior' category in 1992.

The 'yes' vote also drew on the most traditional of variables when it comes to voting for the right: being old. So 55 per cent of pensioners voted for the measure.

So-called 'exit polls' capture only the class and the age of the voters. The Maastricht map reveals that the 'yes' vote also had a strong religious, or rather post-religious, dimension. The Paris region, being the capital city of senior executives, did indeed vote 'yes' in huge numbers. But the traditionally Catholic peripheral provinces also clearly supported the single currency, as is shown in Map 1.4. A coefficient of correlation of +0.47 still links the 'yes' vote in 1992 with the residual Catholic practice measured by IFOP in 2009.

(We should note that a linear coefficient of correlation between two series of figures can vary from between −1 to +1. The positive or negative link between the two series gets closer as the absolute value of the coefficient approaches 1.)

Note too that that the variables of class and religion are not absolutely independent, as the upper strata of society still show a more significant residual practice of religion than the lower classes. The bourgeoisie, Voltairean at the end of the eighteenth century, had become partly re-Catholicized in

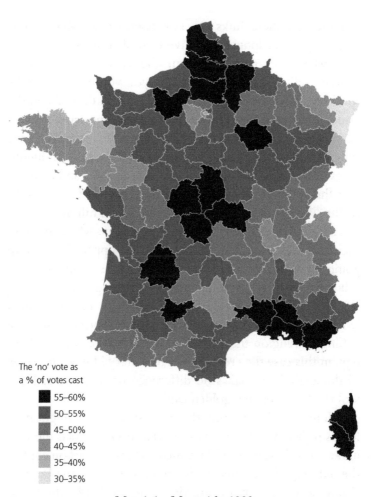

The 'no' vote as
a % of votes cast

■ 55–60%
■ 50–55%
■ 45–50%
■ 40–45%
■ 35–40%
□ 30–35%

Map 1.4   Maastricht 1992

the nineteenth, including in the de-Christianized part of the
national territory. Fear of a social revolution is the reason
for this renewed interest in the succour of religion. We can
likewise point to a relation between age and religion, since
a certain religious practice, as we have seen, subsists among
the over-65s, and especially among the over-75s.

However, these links are not essential, as what counts these days is no longer an active Catholicism. And it would be mistaken to conclude from the correlations between residual religious practice and the 'yes' vote that, generally speaking, it is the vote of 'Catholics' who, in the wake of the senior executives, led France into the awe-inspiring mysteries of the single currency. I myself made this mistake at the time. I noticed the coincidence between the maps of religious practice around 1960 and the 'yes' vote in 1992 and deduced that the votes for Maastricht had been cast by Catholics. In reality, if we bear in mind the statistically significant masses, it is the vote of electors from Catholic milieus who had nonetheless *already abandoned Catholicism* that tipped France into going for the Treaty. So the option for the single currency followed – swiftly, for a historian of the long duration – the abandoning of the single God. It was not religion which led to support for a particular economic project; it was the ebbing of religion that led to its being *replaced* by an ideology, in this case the creation of a monetary idol: at this stage of the analysis, it makes no difference whether we call this idol the 'euro' or the 'golden calf'.

Admittedly, just putting the maps side by side might have led us to believe that the 'yes' to Maastricht echoed the vote in favour of Giscard in 1974, which itself was a carbon copy of the old map of the conservative right, evident in the Popular Front elections of 1936, and visible before 1914. The incessant appearances made by Valéry Giscard d'Estaing on the pro-Maastricht platforms of the campaign bolstered this illusion. But it was really the recently de-Christianized masses that allowed monetary utopia to win out in 1992, just as they had fostered the renaissance of the Socialist Party after 1965 and its rise to power, first on the left, and then in France as a whole. The map of the growth of the Socialist Party between 1965 and 1990 also resembles the map of Catholicism.

François Hollande, the left and zombie Catholicism

Over the three decades that led up to Maastricht, the essential dynamics of the French politico-ideological system had consisted in a shift towards the left on the part of the right-wing Catholic electorate. The significance of this phenomenon is not just a matter of statistics. Its kinetic energy gave the group an attacking advantage. It produced new faces and new ideas. The CFTC lost its religious affiliations and became the CFDT; the left mark-II won out over the left mark-I, which remained old-style secularist, faithful to a ritualized version of socialism. It was this movement that led to Maastricht. The way class structure determined voting patterns should not lead us to forget that monetary utopia was a socialist utopia followed, with various degrees of enthusiasm, by the right. Never would the conservative party of Giscard or the RPR of Jacques Chirac have had the energy, the creativity – in a word, the faith – that were necessary for inventing the single currency.

In *Le Mystère français*, which I co-wrote with Hervé Le Bras,[1] we gave the name 'zombie Catholicism' to the anthropological and social force that emerged from the final disintegration of the Church in its traditional bastions. I will later be examining other phenomena, in education and the economy, which provide evidence of the survival of this residual form after the death of the peripheral Catholic subculture. This cultural survival is probably the most important social phenomenon of the years from 1965 to 2015. It eventually led France into a multifaceted ideological venture, including the rise of a new kind of socialism, decentralization, a surge of pro-European feeling, a masochistic monetary

---

[1] Hervé Le Bras and Emmanuel Todd, *Le Mystère français* (Paris: Seuil and La République des idées, 2013).

policy, a deformation of the nature of the Republic and, as we shall later see, a particularly shitty form of Islamophobia and, probably, of anti-Semitism.

François Hollande, the son of a Catholic doctor from the far right, and a mother who was a left-wing Catholic social worker, is the perfect embodiment of this zombie Catholicism. It could even be considered to be the ideal type, in Weber's sense, of the zombie Catholic. The man doubtless thinks of himself as being on the left, and would find it difficult to admit that his deepest values remain those of his childhood: hierarchy, obedience and maybe matriarchy. The latest form of Catholicism was, after all, a religion of the mother, based on the cult of the Virgin Mary, especially in the west of France.

This quick glance at the president's religious ID explains a great deal. Elected to head a nation in a difficult situation, the president persists in doing nothing, not making any decisions, not being great, remaining humble, in line with his upbringing. But this was precisely the mentality that, in its original version, allowed Catholics in the French army not to disobey the Republic too much during the Dreyfus Affair, and meant the chiefs of staff of the navy felt able to scuttle the French fleet in Toulon on 27 November 1942. It is sometimes claimed that the current resident of the Elysée Palace is indecisive because of his radical socialist roots, but this is not true: his hesitations are indeed cultural and collective, but are actually only one of the virtual aspects of the Catholic subculture that has been magnificently transmitted to that archetypal Catholic zombie François Hollande. Like so many others before him, he is dust, and unto dust he shall return.

To understand the way the French political system has so spectacularly broken down, we now need to answer a fundamental question: what exactly is the nature of the Socialist

Party that has been revitalized by the absorption of refugees from Catholicism? We have fallen into the habit of passing comment only on politics as a conscious and explicit activity, and this has long led us to believe that right-wing regions were moving to the left. But anthropology allows us to grasp the unconscious factors that define the groups and individuals that comprise these regions. Thus it invites us to adopt a more realistic representation of the choices they make. As we have noted, Catholicism was deeply rooted in regions where family structures were reluctant to admit the principle of equality. Is it not likely that zombie Catholics, in joining the Socialist Party rather than converting to the egalitarianism of the central regions, have brought their inegalitarian mental baggage with them and deposited it in the heart of the left? Do we not here hold the key element explaining, first, the way the Socialist Party has been soft on the banks, and, second, its endlessly reiterated, manic support for order and austerity?

The strong franc, the march to the euro, the achievement of the euro: all continue to torture the social body and erode democracy. The Socialist Party may even be becoming more insensitive and harsh towards the weak than the conservative right used to be. Social Catholicism did at least despise money and encouraged the privileged to feel a sense of responsibility towards the poor. The Socialist cult of the single currency takes us beyond a Catholic conception of society.

2005: a missed opportunity in class struggle?

The 2005 referendum on the European Constitutional Treaty showed a strengthening of the vertical or class dimension of the vote that led to its being rejected by some 55 per cent of

voters. Only 19 per cent of workers voted 'yes', as opposed
to 40 per cent of employees. The 'yes' vote among artisans
and small shopkeepers almost stayed the same; indeed, at 45
per cent, it was one point higher than it had been in 1992.
Conversely, the intermediate professions clearly shifted
into the 'no' camp, with just 46 per cent voting 'yes'. There
was an 8 per cent decline in the number of managerial and
liberal professions who supported the project, but 62 per
cent of them still voted 'yes' to the Treaty. As for the zombie
Catholic vote, those who voted 'yes' showed a sharp decline
in numbers: while the few peripheral *départements* that rati-
fied the treaty were all zombie Catholic in complexion, the
overall geographical correlation between residual Catholic
practice and the 'yes' vote fell to +0.36.

The most surprising thing here is the hardening of pro-
European opinion in the well-off parts of the Paris region.
In Paris itself, the 'yes' vote rose from 62.5 per cent to 66.5
per cent; in the Yvelines, from 57.4 to 59.5 per cent; in the
Hauts-de-Seine from 56.7 to 61.9 per cent. On the other
hand, the rest of the Île-de-France just about slipped over
into the 'no' camp. Amongst students, 54 per cent voted
'yes': there was no place on the agenda for any supposedly
revolutionary fervour among the educated youth of 2005.

The vote of pensioners, as befits the age group concerned,
did not shift in the slightest: it was 56 per cent. This was
a rise of just 1 per cent: apparently, ideological arthritis
progresses only slowly.

And so, as far as the majority of the population was concerned, it was clear by 2005 that the European project had
failed. But one could also observe a greater inflexibility, a
hardening, in the attachment shown by the privileged classes
for this utopia. And it would be wrong to think of this loyalty
solely in the simplistic terms of economic self-interest. Of
course, the bastion of pro-European resistance is made up of

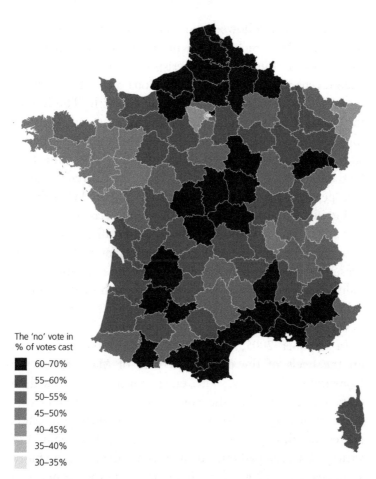

The 'no' vote in
% of votes cast

■ 60–70%
■ 55–60%
■ 50–55%
■ 45–50%
■ 40–45%
■ 35–40%
■ 30–35%

Map 1.5   Constitutional Treaty 2005

people who suffer the least from the economic shipwreck of
the Eurozone, either because their access to capital protects
them, and they can draw on its financial benefits, or because
they have colonized the state, which guarantees their job
security. But we must not ignore the metaphysical dimension of this fixation. The monetary utopia had emerged
from the collapse of the Catholic religion just as the French

Revolution had followed the first wave of de-Christian-ization and Nazism had been produced by the collapse of Protestantism. But the current crisis is also setting in motion deep mechanisms of an almost religious order. It is difficult for believers to abandon their monetary faith. The loss of the meaning of things is particularly serious, even painful, for those who are supposedly defining the future of a society and guiding it in its quest of a better life. After the One God and his paradise, there was the Single Currency and its Europe, but after the Single Currency – what? What dream will guide their footsteps now? The ruling class is suffering. But at this point we need to be more specific: it should be clear that the ruling class's rigid monetarist faith does not presuppose any deep attachment to its values on the part of individuals. Quite the opposite: the strength of the group's belief follows from the weakness of the belief of individuals, as we shall be seeing later.

In October 2005, an uprising in the suburbs followed on the heels of the class-based vote of May against the Constitutional Treaty. The elites swiftly agreed, with a certain elegance, that the youths who were torching cars were, at worst, just badly brought-up French youngsters expressing, through this vandalism, their desire to be part of society. This sympathetic attitude seems archaic today but it shows us that, in 2005, Islamophobia had not yet penetrated the French middle classes.

The fact remains that at the end of 2005, a decidedly rather unsettling year for the ruling classes, it might have been possible to sense that France was going to resume the good old class struggle. But what became clear in 2015, after ten years in which Islamophobia had spread through the middle classes and anti-Semitism through the suburbs, was that France had not opted for economic confrontation. The religious, or quasi-religious, factor that in 2005 seemed to be fading away had made a come-back. But zombie Catholicism, imperious and zestful but still in a minority, cannot be held solely responsible for the mentally unbalanced state that is gradually pervading French society.

Difficult atheism

We should not at present underestimate the way the secular heart of France has contributed to the religious malaise that is gradually but irresistibly on the rise. These days, it is getting more difficult to be an atheist. *La France centrale*,[1] the France of unbelievers, had not been completely abandoned by the Church between 1791 and 1960. Here, the Church existed in a negative mode – as an enemy, of course, but as a reliable metaphysical reference point, a pole to be avoided. Unbelievers defined themselves as free thinkers, escapees from the theological prison, glad to have recovered their liberty. So long as a clerical adversary was still around, the godless were protected from having to face up to ultimate questions. After religious belief, what comes next? Basically, of course, the answer is: modern political ideologies. De-Christianized France has seen a succession of movements: the Revolution, the republican left (the real

---

[1] This is a phrase the author uses to refer, not to 'central France' in a geographical sense, but to a France that includes the Paris Basin, slimmed down and extended southwards, covering a swathe of territory from Laon in the northeast to Bordeaux in the southwest, plus the Mediterranean seafront, but definitely excluding the Massif Central. As he explains, this is the France of liberty and equality, marked from the eighteenth century onwards, to various degrees, by egalitarian nuclear family structures and/ or de-Christianization. *La France centrale* combines geographical, cultural and historical dimensions: it is based on the Paris region and defines the central axis of French history – Capetian, revolutionary, republican and anarchist. Having consulted the author, I have decided to keep *la France centrale* to refer to this complex notion. (Translator's note.)

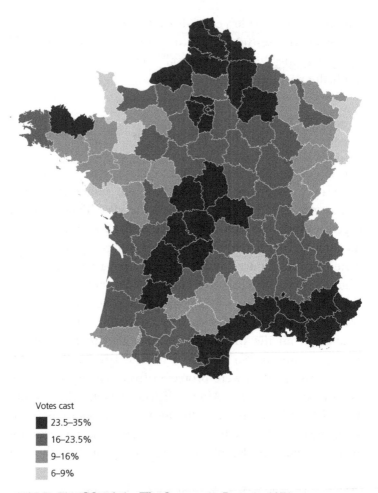

Votes cast
- ■ 23.5–35%
- ■ 16–23.5%
- ■ 9–16%
- ■ 6–9%

Map 1.6   The Communist Party in 1973

one) and, finally, the Communist Party, the apotheosis of the
cartographical coincidence between a left-wing force and de-
Christianization (Map 1.6). In its maturity, after the Second
World War, the Communist vote fitted into French territory as an almost perfect negative of religious practice, with
a few exceptions such as the Côtes d'Armor, a highly original

département on the anthropological level, occupied as it is in its western areas by a communitarian and matrilocal family type. But the geographical complementarity of Catholic and Communist regions suggests a structure, a system, not to say a complicity. From 1789 to 1981, the revolutionary ideas of the centre of France and the Mediterranean seafront seem almost to rely on the Catholic bastions of the periphery.

The image that springs to mind is the rather unexpected one of a revolutionary nave stabilized by Catholic flying buttresses. Are we so sure that, at any given moment, the revolutionary idea could have existed through its own strength, without the support of its Catholic contradiction?

The final disappearance of the Church has left a great void in the lives of secular French people. The end of Catholicism was also a crisis for secular France. We cannot fail to be struck by the way the fall of the Communist Party *followed* the decline of religious practice. It was in 1981 that the vote for the French Communist Party abruptly dropped from 20.6 per cent to 15.3 per cent, about a decade before the implosion of the Soviet system, but after fifteen years of decline in Catholicism.

Until the collapse of religion in its peripheral provinces in the west, the western Pyrenees, the south and the east of the Massif Central, the Rhône-Alpes region, the Jura, Lorraine, Alsace and the extreme north of France, secularism had never needed to define itself in the absolute terms of a godless world. It had been happy just to play the role of the opposition. From the early 1990s, the fundamental problem of unbelief could finally start to emerge. The non-existence of God, a completely reasonable idea, does not solve the question of the ultimate aims of human existence. Atheism succeeds only in defining a meaningless world and a human race without a project. So secular France is contributing in its own way to the new religious malaise. Not because France needs to get used to unbelief, but because it finally has to experience it 'in absolute terms', deprived of the moral and psychological resources of anticlerical protest.

As for Catholic zombie France, it is finally moving, abruptly, into the boundless void of a godless and atheist world. The term is here taken in its neutral sense, without reference to any militant dimension (the concept of agnosticism does not strike me as sociologically relevant). The wealth of possible interactions between the old atheism and the new atheism seems limitless, but difficult to analyse in the absence of data from surveys that might distinguish between the two metaphysical voids. It seems reasonable to imagine the worst. The combination of two anxieties cannot reasonably produce a sense of well-being. An effect of mutual and circular reinforcement can easily be envisaged.

If we agree that atheism, far from generating a long-term, unadulterated sense of psychological well-being, instead produces anxiety, we should imagine the population of France as being in a state of metaphysical danger. At this stage of our analysis, we should even depict it as being in quest of a structuring enemy, a target. Islam fits the bill, both in our French suburbs, disorganized as they are by the crisis in advanced capitalism, and in Islam's own countries of origin, which are overwhelmed by the crises brought on by their transition to modernity. Without ignoring the very real existence of Muslim fundamentalism or terrorism, we have to be able to admit that if the France of unbelievers is to regain its balance, it will need a scapegoat to replace its own Catholicism, which has become unusable.

The demonization of Islam is a response to the intrinsic need of a completely de-Christianized society. Without this hypothesis, we will fail to understand why millions of secular French people marched behind their zombie Catholic president on behalf of the absolute right to caricature

Muhammad, a religious figure respected by at best 5 per cent of France's inhabitants – and these among the weakest and most vulnerable in the country.

Of course, this model cannot tell us which of the two forms of French secularism, the old one or the new one, was most active in the 11 January demonstrations. But the statistical analysis of the demonstrations will enable us to give this question a simple answer. And this is how we will discover who Charlie really is; indeed, better than that: we will recognize him behind his new disguise.

2

Charlie

Immediately after the huge demonstrations of 11 January, the press was full of maps and charts estimating, city by city, the number of participants. The haste in which they were drawn up, in an atmosphere of republican self-celebration, guarantees that they contain a great many errors.

It was claimed that the number of demonstrators, in relation to the active population alone, was higher than 25 per cent in thirty cities, with Cherbourg holding the record: 57 per cent. It would be easy to wax ironical over this and propose that we (at least) halve all the estimates, and perhaps even sketch out a theory of the statistical effects of the media's longing for unanimity. But it would a mistake to think that these figures are worthless. The spread of intensities across national territory intersects with the spread of other variables. Also, statistical theory tells us that when the errors in a set of figures are random, i.e. do not result from any systematic bias, the correlation measured is lower than what it would have been if the measure had been precise. In other terms, if the size of the demonstrations was determined by one or several causes, errors in recording the figures will play against the statistical emergence of these causes. In short, if we manage to draw one or more laws from these hastily cobbled-together figures, we can be sure that this law, or these laws, are actually more powerful than the data suggest.

We have no reason to suspect the tandem 'Ministry of the Interior/*Libération*' of having introduced a systematic bias. The figures are exaggerated, certainly, but in a random way. However, I have here used the data given by *Libération* on 12 January only for the eighty-five most populous cities. For small cities and towns, the tendency to swell the figures, to 'indicate that something happened', becomes irresistible – a dramatization, as it were, of the Cherbourg effect of inflated numbers. Map 2.1 includes the 10 January demonstrations, on the eve of the great day, when they were recorded by *Libération*. I have added them to the 11 January events when two demonstrations followed each other in the same city, as in Marseilles. Of course, some individuals may have demonstrated on two days in succession, but it would have been unfair not to reward statistically the energy that was thereby expended. In the case of Paris, where the figures given range between 1.5 and 2 million demonstrators, I have played devil's advocate and opted for the higher estimate. If no estimate has been given for any one of the eighty-five cities, I have counted a minimal number of demonstrators – a thousand – and, in the case of Douai-Lens, ignored on the map, a figure of zero demonstrators.

In 2015, these eighty-five metropolitan areas include 41.2 million residents, i.e. 63 per cent of the population of France. The total number of demonstrators recorded was 4,394,000. Thus the average proportion of demonstrators was 10.7 for every 100 inhabitants in the main French cities, with the average rate being just 7.5 per cent. The size of the Parisian

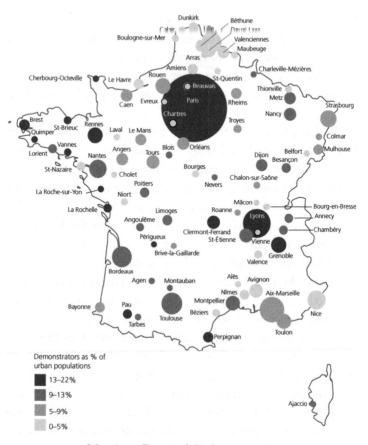

Map 2.1   Extent of the demonstrations

conurbation – 12 million residents – is the main explanation for this divergence: its rate of 16.3 per cent, one of the
highest, swells the average of the rates less than its 2 million
demonstrators swell the average rate.

In French towns and cities, one person in ten identified
with Charlie – a considerable number. However, the figures
varied widely across national territory. The size of the city
does not seem to have played much part: a correlation of
+0.20, or +0.14 if we exclude Paris.

Table 2.1

Metropolitan area	Population (2011)	Number of demonstrators (1000s)	Rate per 100 inhabitants
Cherbourg	116 878	25	21.4
Brest	314 239	65	20.7
Rennes	679 866	125	18.4
Saint-Brieuc	170 779	30	17.6
Grenoble	675 122	110	16.3
Paris	12 292 895	2 000	16.3
Quimper	124 930	20	16.0
La Roche-sur-Yon	116 856	18	15.4
Clermont-Ferrand	467 178	70	15.0
Périgueux	101 773	15	14.7
La Rochelle	205 822	30	14.6
Pau	240 898	35	14.5
Lyons	2 188 759	300	13.7
Vannes	149 312	20	13.4
Perpignan	305 546	40	13.1
Tarbes	116 056	15	12.9
Bordeaux	1 140 668	140	12.3
Toulouse	1 250 251	150	12.0
Blois	126 814	15	11.8
Saint-Étienne	508 548	60	11.8
Agen	111 011	13	11.7
Metz	389 529	45	11.6
Nancy	434 565	50	11.5
Charleville-Mézières	106 440	12	11.3
Angoulême	179 540	20	11.1
Montpellier	561 326	60	10.7
Poitiers	254 051	27	10.6

Table 2.1 (continued)

Metropolitan area	Population (2011)	Number of demonstrators (1000s)	Rate per 100 inhabitants
Limoges	282 876	30	10.6
Montauban	104 534	11	10.5
Besançon	245 178	25	10.2
Ajaccio	100 621	10	9.9
Nevers	102 447	10	9.8
Lorient	214 066	20	9.3
Dijon	375 841	35	9.3
Chambéry	216 528	20	9.2
Annecy	219 470	20	9.1
Nantes	884 275	80	9.0
Mulhouse	282 714	25	8.8
Roanne	107 392	9	8.4
Rheims	315 480	25	7.9
Colmar	127 598	10	7.8
Chalon-sur-Saône	133 298	10	7.5
Angers	400 428	30	7.5
Caen	401 208	30	7.5
Tours	480 378	35	7.3
Bayonne	283 571	20	7.1
Brive-la-Gaillarde	101 915	7	6.9
Aix-Marseille	1 720 941	115	6.7
Toulon	606 987	40	6.6
Troyes	190 179	12	6.3
Strasbourg	764 013	45	5.9
Le Mans	343 175	20	5.8
Rouen	655 013	35	5.3
Orléans	421 047	22	5.2
Saint-Nazaire	211 675	10	4.7
Laval	121 017	5	4.1

Table 2.1 (continued)

Metropolitan area	Population (2011)	Number of demonstrators (1000s)	Rate per 100 inhabitants
Valence	175 195	7	4.0
Niort	152 148	6	3.9
Arras	128 989	5	3.9
Lille	1 159 547	40	3.4
Bourges	139 368	4	2.9
Cholet	104 742	3	2.9
Nice	1 003 947	28	2.8
Calais	126 308	3	2.4
Dunkirk	257 887	6	2.3
Le Havre	291 579	5	1.7
Amiens	293 646	5	1.7
Valenciennes	367 998	3	0.8
Béthune	367 924	3	0.7
Mâcon	100 172	1	1.0
Évreux	110 661	1	0.9
Saint-Quentin	111 549	1	0.9
Vienne	111 606	1	0.9
Alès	112 741	1	0.9
Belfort	113 507	1	0.9
Bourg-en-Bresse	121 386	1	0.8
Beauvais	124 603	1	0.8
Maubeuge	129 872	1	0.8
Boulogne-sur-Mer	132 661	1	0.8
Thionville	134 736	1	0.7
Chartres	146 142	1	0.7
Béziers	162 430	1	0.6
Nîmes	256 205	1	0.4
Avignon	515 123	1	0.2
Douai–Lens	542 946	0	0.0

Note: Towns and cities in **bold** are mainly Catholic

Charlie: middle-class and zombie Catholics

A comparison between the number of demonstrators with the social composition of the cities is highly revealing. Maps 2.2 and 2.3 show, respectively, the proportions of 'manual workers' and 'managerial and professional workers' in each metropolitan area.

It is easy to locate the low rates in towns and cities with a high proportion of manual workers, such as Dunkirk,

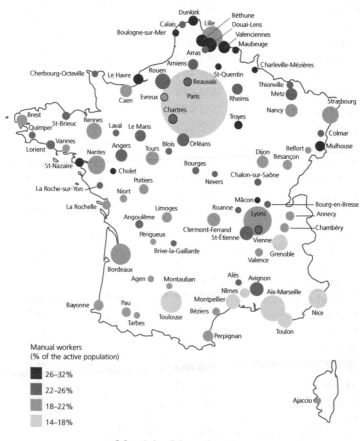

Map 2.2   *Manual workers*

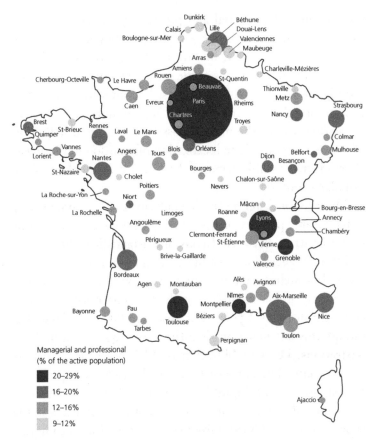

Managerial and professional
(% of the active population)

- 20–29%
- 16–20%
- 12–16%
- 9–12%

Map 2.3   Middle classes

Amiens, Saint-Quentin, Maubeuge, Charleville-Mézières, Thionville, Rouen, Le Havre, Mulhouse, Belfort, Laval, Le Mans and Cholet. At the other end of the spectrum, the citadels of executives, Paris first and foremost, followed by Lyons, Bordeaux, Toulouse, Rennes and Nantes display a higher intensity of mobilization.

We can measure a correlation of –0.45 between the rate of demonstrators and the proportion of manual workers, and one of +0.38 between the rate of demonstrators and the proportion of managerial and professional workers.[1] These two indices may not be very high, but they are, from the statistical point of view, highly significant. We should bear in mind the imperfections of the measurement, and also note the higher coefficient for workers. It points to an indifference among the working class that is even more decisive than the enthusiasm of the middle class, as far as the distribution of intensities goes.[2] The localization of emotion in the lower classes is more reminiscent of the Dreyfus Affair than of the Popular Front.

There is one significant irregularity that is immediately striking, and puts us on the track of religious factors: this is the contrast between Lyons and Marseilles, the second and third biggest conurbations in France respectively. Here, Marseilles includes its 'bourgeois' part, with a large number of students and academics, namely Aix. There were 300,000 demonstrators in Lyons, but just 115,000 in Marseilles, though this last figure amalgamates two days' worth of demonstrations, i.e. a mobilization of 13.7 per cent as against 6.7 per cent. The contrast between the two metropolises is almost always meaningful because each of them is the heart of a cultural region with its own identity. Marseilles is the capital of the de-Christianized southeast, and used to have a strong Communist presence, while these days it has a large number of National Front voters. Lyons is the capital of the traditionally Catholic Rhône-Alpes region. These two cities embody respectively the urban metamorphoses of old secularism and zombie Catholicism. The contrast between them

---

[1] The probability of making a mistake by rejecting the hypothesis of a null effect of the rate of workers in a city on the rate of its demonstrators is less than 5 out of 1,000 (p-value = 0.00451).
[2] A multiple linear regression confirms that the rate among executives does not in fact play any significant role, once we have checked the rate among workers and the level of Catholic influence in an area.

leads one to suspect that the populations of the Catholic periphery have a strong tendency to demonstrate, while those in the regions of longstanding de-Christianization are reluctant to make the effort to turn out.

We can treat the question in overall terms, classifying the cities in terms of the either Catholic or old-secular preponderance in their regional environment. In certain cases, very few and far between, I have had to resort to an intermediary category. Map 2.4 divides cities into three categories: a strong,

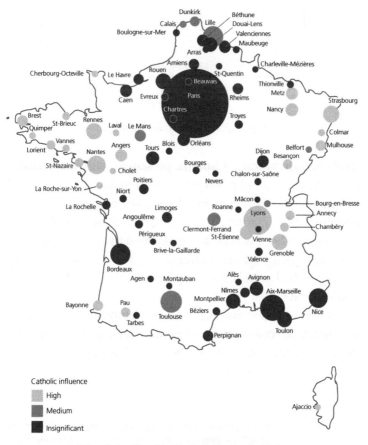

Map 2.4   Zombie Catholicism in the cities

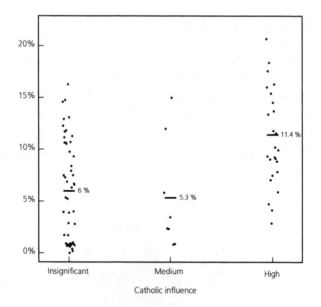

Figure 2.1   Rate of demonstrators

weak or insignificant Catholic presence. This map derives from the maps of religious practice presented in the previous chapter for the *départements*. I have taken into account the main flow of migrations in assessing the religious background of the cities. So it is here being assumed that provincial cities have absorbed regional cultures at the same time as they have absorbed populations displaced by the exodus from the countryside.

As we see, the average rate of demonstrators was, on average, 6 per cent in the traditionally secular cities, and 11.4 per cent in the zombie Catholic cities; here again, there is a clear correlation, close to that measured for workers, namely +0.43.[1]

---

[1] The probability of making a mistake by rejecting the hypothesis of a null effect of the 'strong Catholic presence' in a city on its rate of demonstrators is less than 2 out of 100,000 (p-value = 1.51×10^{-5}).

Neo-republicanism

The demonstrations drew mainly on the upper half of French society and its post-Catholic periphery: so the result needs to be viewed as the *hegemony* of a bloc or a social coalition rather than as a show of unanimity. The lower-class milieu were reduced to silence, as were the descendants of immigrants in the suburbs, who were mainly absent from the demonstrations, as all the commentators eventually agreed. The Republic that was being defended was not a Republic of all citizens. An anthropological and geographical understanding of French society will force us to admit that the new doctrines – pro-European as well as recent republican mentalities – are supported by the classes and regions that are least faithful, or not at all faithful, to the principle of equality. This will explain why, during the demonstrations, we did not hear much about the second term in the republican slogan, namely 'equality'.

To avoid any confusion, I will henceforth use the term 'neo-republicanism' to refer to the doctrine that is emerging, which manically emphasizes its devotion to Marianne and secularism but actually finds that its most reliable support comes from those Catholic regions that resisted the establishment of the Republic most vigorously. Statistical analysis leads us to the following basic question: *Why are the regions that now support the European project and secularism most fervently the same regions that, when they were Catholic, provided the anti-Dreyfus campaign with its biggest battalions, and the Vichy regime with its firmest supporters?*

There is an optimistic answer to this question. The final decline of Catholicism in its bastions among the upper classes and the peripheral areas of France could perhaps have led to a complete emancipation of the groups concerned, and a sincere and deep-rooted attachment to the values of

In actual fact, just listing the cities in decreasing order of the proportions taking part in the demonstrations shows a zombie Catholic effect. At the top come in order: Cherbourg, Brest, Rennes, Saint-Brieuc, Grenoble, Paris, Quimper and La Roche-sur-Yon. The west is overrepresented – this is, as it were, the signature of Catholicism here, a belated and peculiar homage to the *Tableau politique de la France de l'Ouest*, that masterpiece of French political science in which, in 1913, André Siegfried studied the role of Catholicism in the ineradicable right-wing tendencies of the west of France. His analysis was of crucial importance for the republicans of his day. It told them that they would have to learn to live with the Church. But these days, what we need to grasp is why the west of France rose up *in the name of republican values* – a miraculous change, if indeed we accept that they were defending *the same* Republic as the one that was so hated there between 1791 and 1914.

However, the zombie Catholic effect is absent from the cities with a large working-class population, such as Laval, Angers, Cholet and Saint-Nazaire. With the exception of Saint-Nazaire, the cities in the west of France are rarely perceived as 'working class' because their industries have been established there only recently. These days, the economic maps of France mainly register the collapse of the industrial workforce that has resulted from the crazy policy mix that for thirty years has combined free trade and a strong currency. The cities in the west of France have resisted more effectively, and now appear to have proportions of workers as great as the hard-hit cities of the north and east of the Paris Basin. Indeed, the lower Loire region until recently witnessed considerable dynamism, fostered by new industries, often electronic but always diversified. Cholet is well known for its network of inventive enterprises, but the discreet city of Laval is just as remarkable.

Strasbourg is missing from the cities where there was a high proportion of demonstrators: the reason for this is not to be sought in its working- and lower-class ambiance. Strasbourg, the capital of Alsace, is a major administrative and university city, well stocked with executives and members of the liberal professions. But we should at this point remember the main theme of the demonstration, one that was explicit for some people, implicit or even unconscious for others: 'I am Charlie, I am French, I have the right and even the duty to blaspheme against the Islam of others as well as against my own Catholicism.' The two *départements* of Alsace and Moselle were part of Germany between 1871 and 1918 and did not experience the separation of Church and State in 1905. They are still under the Concordat of 1801, which does not recognize the right to blasphemy. Jean-Luc Mélenchon, with his absurd sense for historical priorities, thought that the law on blasphemy should be applied to this particular region, long before the *Charlie Hebdo* affair. Alsaciens have their own specific relation to religion. Its inhabitants still sometimes identify themselves as Catholics or Protestants. Without in the least claiming that the low number of demonstrators in Strasbourg reveals any particular affection for Islam, we can agree that the ideological axis of the 11 January demonstrations did not really suit the cultural dynamics of Alsace. I will come back later to the dramatic consequences that the new secularist hysteria could have in Alsace.

So a detailed analysis of the demonstrations does not lead to the discovery of a new, regenerated, recreated world. The demonstrators were stirred into action for basically the same reasons as those who voted for Maastricht. The most motivated social strata were the middle classes from the public and the private sectors, with a large component of zombie Catholics enriching the mix in the provinces.

The regression on the three variables – the propor tion of workers, the proportion of managerial and libe professions, and the Catholic influence – 'explains', in statistical sense, 40 per cent of the variance in the proporti of demonstrators.[1] Given the uncertainty of the data, thi remarkable. The error term between the proportion to approached and the values predicted by the model inclu not just – as one would expect – absent explanatory variab but also a massive error in measurement. Without this er the level of determination would probably be of the orde 55 per cent.

In the parallel with Maastricht, only senior citizens are present. We have not included them in our analysis beca it is clear that above a certain age it becomes more diffi to take part in a demonstration. However, it is certain the citizens who did demonstrate were on average ra elderly, if compared with revolutionary crowds. It inclu a far from negligible number of pensioners.

So Charlie is an old acquaintance. The social forces expressed their opinion on 11 January are the same ones had voted the treaty of Maastricht into being. The e tions stirred by the killings of 11 January brought bac life not the Republic, but the coalition that had voted its dissolution in the new European order. The masses demonstrated suggest that the 'intermediary' categori the socio-professional labels of the INSEE, the categ that abandoned the coalition in 2005, returned to the ologically dominant bloc of French society in 2015. return resulted in a feeling of unanimity.

[1] The coefficient of determination (R^2 = the proportion of variance proportion of demonstrators that can be explained by the model) is

liberty and equality. (I am here supposing that the value of fraternity is shared by both the Church and the Republic, so I will not mention it as a distinguishing feature of either.)

By depicting the situation in the terms of conversion – a sort of road to Damascus experience in which the Republic becomes the new object of veneration – we could perhaps view the new passion for secularism on the part of groups that have just abandoned the Church, those that were the last to free themselves from the grip of the clergy, as a pure and simple revitalization of traditional secularism. But this turns out not to be the case: far from it – the last stage in the disappearance of Catholicism as a social power did not involve any explicit and violent rejection of the Church, of the kind observed at the time of Voltaire, the French Revolution and the separation of Church and State in 1905. The explicitly Catholic trade union, the CFTC, turned into the secularized CFDT gently and peacefully, without becoming anticlerical in the process.

In fact, before we start indulging in metaphysical speculations on human liberty, we need to accept the way the world actually is, and the importance of the factor of continuity. Neither individuals nor groups can be liberated from their values, either in France or elsewhere, by just thirty years' worth of evolution. The principle of inertia means that a society or a class cannot escape that quickly from the course of its history.

These values are, of course, disguised and unconscious. But we can accept their persistence, and the way they may come into conflict with the conscious values of politicians or voters – values that are worn out of habit, like old clothes: and we can then analyse more effectively one of the structural characteristics of contemporary French political life, namely a permanent contradiction between what is said and what is done.

1992–2015:
from pro-Europeanism to neo-republicanism

This dual phenomenon is typical of pro-Europeanism. The language of Maastricht was liberal, egalitarian and universalist. All that was needed was to further the creation of a united Europe, an association of free and equal nations living in the perpetual peace of a Kantian order. The grandeur of these principles did not involve downplaying economic efficiency as a justifying factor. The euro was going to ensure our prosperity.

The reality turned out to be the complete opposite. Growth slowed down, there was economic stagnation. Far from leading to the triumph of liberty and equality, Maastricht led to the triumph of inequality under the transcendental authority of a cruel deity: the currency. The iron hand of economic management came down heavily on the lower classes, leading to the destruction of industrial activity and the privileging of financial services. Europe became a hierarchy of unequal nations.

It used to be possible to agree that the politicians and voters in favour of Maastricht were all incompetent, could not imagine the economic consequences of their ideological dreams, and were really thinking in terms of republican liberty and equality. The sudden opposition of ordinary people and the elites in 1992 could be seen as an unfortunate accident, just like the residual Catholicism in the 'yes' vote. But in 2015, the effects of Maastricht are there for all to see. The factories have closed, the suburbs are decaying. And we need to voice the hypothesis that, in the minds of those who dreamed up the single currency, this alone had been the only issue all along: *What is happening is not in contradiction with the values of the social coalition that controls France. Quite the contrary: what is happening is in line with these same values.*

For workers, employees and young people, this has been a wasted quarter of a century. For the ideological debate, too, it has been wasted – wasted in a rhetoric that goes round and round in circles. However, for the analyst, this lapse of time has a certain value in that it finally disclosed the latent values of the protagonists involved. It was an ideal of hierarchy that had led to Maastricht, an ideal that still rules us, rooted as it is in the values of authority and inequality. It comes to us from Catholicism and the Vichy Regime rather than from the Revolution.

Charlie, like Maastricht, works in two ways, the one conscious and positive, liberal and egalitarian and republican, while the other is unconscious and negative, authoritarian and inegalitarian, dominating and excluding.

The 11 January demonstrations were awe-inspiring. It would be a waste of time to go over in detail all the positive things they expressed, in the view of those who took part: the defence of the freedom of expression and secularism, an opening up to 'good Islam' and to the world. But we need only focus our attention on the actual goals of the demonstration to grasp its latent values. It aimed first and foremost at a social power, a form of domination – a goal that was achieved by taking to the streets *en masse*, behind *France*'s government and *France*'s police. The way people identified with the satirical journal *Charlie Hebdo*, meanwhile, powerfully reveals the radical rejection that motivated the demonstrators. The Republic that was being re-established placed the right to blasphemy at the heart of its values, with their immediate point of application being the right to blaspheme against the emblematic person of a *minority* religion, supported by a group that was *discriminated against*. In the context of mass unemployment, in which young people of North African origin find it particularly difficult to find work, and Islam is constantly being demonized by ideologues in high places in French society, on television as in the French Academy, we cannot overemphasize the repressed violence that was present in the 11 January demonstrations.

Millions of French people came out onto the streets to define, as a priority of their society, the right to pour scorn on the religion of the weak. In spite of what they themselves claimed, on this occasion they were not in line with the central axis of their nation's history. Voltaire was often mentioned by Charlie as a doctrinal reference point, as he had been, quite justifiably, by the revolutionaries of 1789 or the supporters of the separation of Church and State in 1905. But if we immerse ourselves in his *Philosophical Dictionary*, what we find is above all an excellent satire on Catholicism, the religion of the author's forefathers, and Judaism, the sole source of this religion. The *Dictionary* takes little interest in Islam or Protestantism. It contains articles on Abraham, David, Jesus, Joseph, Julian, Moses, Paul, Peter and Solomon, but none on Muhammad, Luther or Calvin. Unlike Charlie, Voltaire did not denounce the religion of others. He blasphemed against his own religion and the religion from which that had stemmed.

We do not have enough distance in time from the 2015 demonstration, as we do from Maastricht, for us to able to say as yet that Charlie is going to create an authoritarian and inegalitarian monster. In any case, we do not know how deeply the middle classes of Paris are imbued with the value of inequality – which is absolutely not typical of the Paris region as a whole. It is possible, as I will be showing in later chapters, that the Paris demonstration included a xenophobic element completely independent of the Catholic tradition, one that draws, in quite the opposite way, on the dark face of the revolutionary and republican tradition. So we cannot answer this question: does Charlie have a link with the darkest years of contemporary France?

But in the France of 2015 people are being dragged along by the rise of Islamophobic and anti-Semitic feelings, and we cannot wait until we are 'sure' that neo-republicanism is a form of neo-Vichyism in order to declare that this suggestion is valid – quite simply because, if one day we did manage to be sure, it would probably be too late. Islamophobia would have progressed so far that it would have become as dangerous as the anti-Semitism of the traditional right.

What elements do we have at our disposal, in 2015, to assess the situation?

1 We have the geographical and social ID of the demonstration, with its zombie Catholic bastions: this is something that speaks volumes. It is enough to show up all the bland platitudes about secularism for what they are: empty verbiage. What marched at the head of the demonstrations, in the streets of French cities, was not old-style secularism, but a mutant form of the forces that had once supported the Catholic Church. It is zombie Catholicism that is presenting itself as the front line against Islam, not the Revolution. It proclaims the duty to caricature Muhammad. It proposes that we wage a religious war in a world that no longer believes in God.

2 We have the religious and socioeconomic make-up that was shared by the 11 January demonstrations and the 'yes' vote for Maastricht, which suggests that, like the single currency, Charlie could be a dynamic phenomenon that over time reveals its real basic values ever more clearly: authority and inequality. Charlie is still just a child. What will he be like when he grows up?

Be this as it may, the isomorphism we have identified between Maastricht and Charlie enables us to describe the reality of the French social system. The veil of official, conscious politics has been torn for a second time. The same hegemonic bloc is in charge: it was pro-European and optimistic in 1992; it is in a state of shock and potentially Islamophobic in 2015. Charlie, as a collective social being, is not the whole of France, but he has it firmly in his grip, as his own realm.

The neo-republican reality:
the 'social state' of the middle classes

In 2015, France is not a great and generous nation. Pockets of poverty are springing up; the prisons are ever more crowded. For the only authentic response of the hegemonic bloc we can call MEZ (the Middle classes, the Elderly, and Zombie Catholics) to the piling up of problems is the rapid increase in the number of individuals put in jail by the state: 36,913 people were put behind bars in 1980 and 77,883 in 2014. If we take into account the increase in the French population, from 55 to 65 million, we can see an increase in the rate of incarceration of 7 to 12 per 10,000, i.e. over 70 per cent. These are mainly young men. Before we start worrying about their national or religious backgrounds, we should note the average age of the prisoners: 30.1 years old in 1980, 34.6 in 2014.[1] Furthermore, the tendency to incarceration does not reflect any increase in serious acts of violence: according to the police, the number of homicides fell from 1,171 in 1996 to 682 in 2013. It is the injustice of the world that is filling the prisons.

---

[1] The Department of Penitentiary Administration, *Séries statistiques des personnes placées sous main de justice, 1980–2104.*

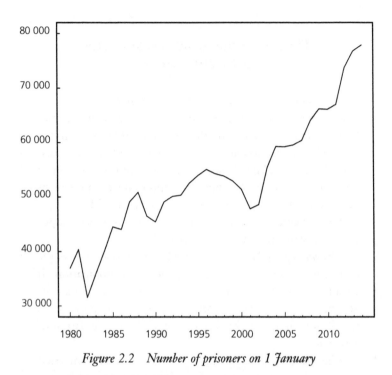

Figure 2.2   Number of prisoners on 1 January

The MEZ bloc continues to express wonderful European and universal values, but in practice it accepts a terrible hardening of attitudes within society. There is no question here of me contesting the traditional French values of liberty and equality, or even of giving a purely negative vision of the MEZ.

In some ways the French middle classes are admirable. Unlike their English, American and German equivalents, they are capable of creating children, in reasonable numbers, and producing cultivated pensioners who flock to art festivals in the summer. They protect our cinema and, generally speaking, preserve a coherent culture in the dislocated culture of globalization. The fact remains that the

The size of the middle classes in the 2010–2015 period

The categories employed by the INSEE allow us to approach the social structure in an empirical way that may be quite inadequate on the theoretical level (as it combines profession, education and income), but is still perfectly reasonable. The middle classes exist, by definition, between an upper class, tiny in size but very important because of its possession of capital, and a vast lower-class world.

Let us begin by leaving to one side the significant population of pensioners and the workless.

The *managing directors* who employ more than ten people constitute barely 0.1 per cent of the active population. If we add the most senior civil servants, the executive managers and the very wealthy *rentiers*, the size of the upper class is still not increased above 1 per cent of the population of active age.

The *workers and employees* – often forming married couples, since 80 per cent of workers are men and 75 per cent of employees are women – comprise the main bulk of the lower and working classes, 50 per cent of the active population. *Artisans* and *small shopkeepers*, 5.5 per cent of the active population, are close to the workers in their educational level and their propensity to vote National Front. They are culturally close to, or even form part of, the lower classes, as are the *rural workers* – 1.5 per cent in total – with the exception of a handful of very large farmers. This gives us a total of 57 per cent for the lower classes in the broad sense of the term.

That leaves, for the middle classes, 42 per cent of the active population. This breaks down into 17 per cent *upper-middle classes* (managerial and liberal professions) and 25 per cent *lower-middle classes* (intermediate professions). Let us imagine, so as to place them relative to each other, the difference between a secondary school teacher and a primary school teacher, or between an engineer and a technician. The first basic thing we learn from this description is that the middle classes constitute a mass that may be smaller than the lower classes but is comparable in size: 42 per cent as against 57 per cent.

It is easy to see how this middle class, combining as it does a higher level of education and a higher income, can control the ideological system.

The second thing we learn is just as important. It is that if the 'upper-middle classes' want to keep the 1 per cent above them and the 57 per cent below them at bay, they need to maintain their hold on the 'lower-middle class'. For since Maastricht, the issue at stake in the ideological struggle is the ideological tendency shown by the lower-middle classes. As far as the lower classes are concerned, they have long since left behind the gravitational field of the upper-middle classes and cannot be brought back into the fold.

Let us not forget, in the balance of social forces, the 32 per cent of pensioners in the population among the over-15s, and the 8 per cent of school children and students.

well-being of this class is the result of a social system that is not just selfish but hypocritical too, since its official representations deny all relations of force, exploitation, exclusion and repression.

The French rhetoric of the 'social state' (*'l'État social'*) is typical. Yes, the French are more fervent supporters of the social state than are the British, and no, they have not, so far, refused to pay the taxes that finance this state. But can we really be sure that what they have in mind is the old social state of the post-war years, the social state that emerged from the struggles of the working class and the long period of ascendancy enjoyed by democratic equality? Admittedly, health care and pensions are still guaranteed for all. This, after all, is the reason for France's excellent performances in health, whether we look at infant mortality or life expectancy. But can we really give the name 'social' to a state whose economic management ensures, structurally and over the long term, a life-destroying unemployment rate of more than 10 per cent? A result of this kind is more reminiscent of the politics of an alliance between castes – a fraternal combination of plutocrats, pensioners and middle classes, both public and private, the MEZ bloc, mostly – that accepts inequality whenever it suits it. Sometimes, indeed, the French state is less social than its Anglo-Saxon equivalent: that latter also includes, as Christophe Ramaux has pertinently emphasized, full employment as one of its long-term objectives. Setting the struggle for employment at the heart of its objectives means, much more than a country with unemployment higher than 10 per cent will admit, accepting the very principle of a social pact, and putting it into application.[1]

But France is also the country where the state, through every sort of activity and programme, specifically advantages those social strata who are already privileged. In the United States, as in Britain, the costs for parents with children in secondary school and higher education are high: this explains the low birth rate in the middle classes. Each child represents a big bill. In France, the situation is the opposite: the state pays the largest share of the cost of secondary and higher education, and this explains why the 'managerial and liberal professions' are demographically healthy: they can procreate without consigning themselves to social suicide. Yes, the

---

[1] Christophe Ramaux, *L'État social* (Paris: Mille et une nuits, 2012).

social state is surviving in France, but mainly because it has become the social state of the middle classes. The dominant discourse now depicts, quite systematically, the middle classes as victims of the taxes they have to pay. In France, depicting them as victims in this way simply expresses the ideological power of the privileged strata of society.[1]

At this point, I would like to avoid any misunderstanding. In my view, it is obvious that the funding of education by the state, i.e. by taxes, is a good thing. Families cannot pay the costs of a long education for their children unaided. And the anti-state dogmatism of the neoliberals might well end up killing what is positive for society in the effective transmission of the cultural achievements of the cultivated strata. The direct heirs of Pierre Bourdieu may refuse to acknowledge the fact, but cultural reproduction is not simply a scandal: it is also a necessity if the continuity of the social system and progress for all are to be ensured. Reproduction is a necessary basis for the widening of education. But all the same, we must not exaggerate. It is extremely cynical to force the lower classes, who live under the menace of a 10 per cent rate of unemployment, to pay for the education of the children of executives. But our information system conceals this reality from us. It does not simply explain to us that Charlie is the whole of France; it goes further, and constantly suggests that the lower classes do not pay any taxes. This is a joke. Indirect taxation – VAT and energy bills – are twice as significant for state revenues than direct taxation, and the least well-off of French people pay more than their fair share, since they need to consume in order to live and thus have to be taxed. But the ideology of the MEZ bloc so dominates the information in circulation that, in 95 per cent of cases, tax on revenue becomes, when economic journalists talk about it, tax as

---

[1] This is not true of British and American society.

much Evit VAT – except, of course, when plans to increase it are mooted, under the Orwellian name of 'social VAT'.

All the same, as I have said, it would be absurd to refuse to see the positive face of the social system that gave birth to Charlie. Neo-republicanism can, after all, claim some notable successes as its own.

The transmutation of the original social state into the 'social state of the middle classes' has put a brake on the widening of economic inequalities. The 'managerial and liberal professions' are subtly protected: they have not sought an answer to the problems they have educating their children by going for hugely inflated incomes. Their British and American equivalents, meanwhile, in their solitude, have lost touch with the lower classes and are themselves fragmented as they attempt to identify with the 1 per cent at the top of the income scale. Year after year, the OECD finds that in France, unlike what can be observed in the other most advanced parts of the world, inequalities of income are not widening, at least between the 80 per cent lower strata and the 19 per cent immediately above them. In France, the top 1 per cent have risen to stratospheric incomes all alone, and they run the risk of becoming ideologically isolated. Is it altogether a coincidence that France has given the world Thomas Piketty, the economist who has targeted the 1 per cent throughout the world? Far from being hateful, the French middle classes still form the solid basis on which we could start to build a really egalitarian and progressive society.

The fact remains that the emergence of Charlie points to the autistic tendency of a social and ideological system of which the '19 per cent', the upper fraction of the middle classes, comprise the centre of gravity. Piketty himself, when he stops being an economist and social scientist and turns to political proposals, for example in the fourth part of his *Capital in the Twenty-First Century*, shows himself to be a perfect pro-European and an authentic neo-republican.[1] His critical vision of the top 1 per cent does not lead him to take the side of the bottom 50 per cent. In this sense, too, he is a product of current French society.

Charlie is anxious

We should not, however, exaggerate the smugness of the MEZ bloc. A metaphysical void is gnawing away at it. Economic uncertainty is pressing in on it, infiltrating it. Its children are growing poorer. Their difficulties in finding a decently paid job and finding somewhere to live affect their parents, not just because the latter love their children, but often because they feel guilty for the way they themselves have had such an easy ride through life.

Some strategic strata in the bloc are fragile. Indian IT is threatening several milieus that are technologically highly competent. The printed press in particular is being rendered obsolescent by the internet; its influence is waning. Its journalists are suffering, belatedly, what the workers in the tyre factories of Picardie suffered: the anxiety that they will see their firm close down before they reach retirement age. When we see *Le Monde* feverishly agitating for month after month in support of a military intervention against the regime of Bashar al-Assad, and then in Ukraine, and when from 3 to 10 February 2015 *L'Express* proclaims on its cover 'The Republic versus Islam', we need to remember that these bellicose press organs are experiencing considerable economic difficulties. Although they are subsidized by

---

[1] Thomas Piketty, *Capital in the Twenty-First Century*, trans. Arthur Goldhammer (Cambridge, MA: The Belknap Press of Harvard University Press, 2014).

the state, they are living under the threat of a new business plan and, perhaps, receivership. The warmongering feverishness of a large proportion of the printed press is also the result, of course, of this threatening economic reality. And if we do not factor this mounting anxiety into the model of analysis of the middle classes, we will fail to understand why Islamophobia has spread through their ranks.

The long-term consequences of the Maastricht project – more than twenty years' worth of failure – thus give us a glimpse of what is, beneath the rhetoric of 'neo-republican parties' who all claim to be loyal to old values, a selfish, unjust and ruthless society. And I need to emphasize that, if we are really to grasp the reality of the French model, we constantly need, in the field of our analysis, to yoke together these two fundamental elements: the liberal and egalitarian doctrinal superstructure handed down from the past, and the authoritarian and inegalitarian mental infrastructure of the present.

The 11 January demonstrations spectacularly reiterated this elementary structure of the French model, but in an aggravated form. The shock unleashed by the horror of the 7 January attacks took France by surprise and allowed hitherto repressed instinctive tendencies to be given free rein. It brought out the start of a drift on the part of the middle classes towards an explicit inegalitarianism, including the designation of a scapegoat.

The rapid examination of the reality of the French model on which we have just embarked now means we can set the demonstrations back in their economic and social context. The tricolour flags and the statues of Marianne that we saw on 11 January should not deceive us. On that day, we swam in the deep waters of inequality, and not at all in those of republican equality. The recreation of the republic was a deformation, a subversion, a violation of history – the very definition of a neo-republicanism of exclusion. And, that day, the new ideological system was supported by the middle classes, who wanted to state loudly and clearly that they scorned being concerned by the social disintegration created by their selfishness. Are pro-Europeanism and the euro destroying a whole swathe of our young population, and not just those in the suburbs? Too bad: 'our values' are good and true; they are the only 'real values'.

At this stage, it is quite easy to understand what was apparently the main contradiction of the demonstrations, which had been called out to support an 'anarchist' paper, but which spontaneously acclaimed the state and its police.

The size of the marches, even when deflated from the exaggerated figures provided by the media, leaves us in no doubt about the way the upper-middle classes managed to persuade many people from the lower strata of the urban social structure to follow them. The 'managerial and liberal professions' comprise only 20 per cent of the active French population – 28 per cent in Paris, 24 per cent in Toulouse, 20 per cent in Lyons and Lille, 19 per cent in Rennes and Marseilles, and 18 per cent in Bordeaux. Rates of support of over 100 per cent would have been necessary to bring together the crowds observed. We admittedly need to accept, initially at least, the assumption that the middle classes came out in exceptional numbers, and that this revealed a state of feverish disquiet of a kind that did not exist at the time of Maastricht with its tranquil consciences. But on that 11 January 2015, the upper echelons of French society mainly demonstrated a renewed capacity to persuade broad swathes of the lower-middle classes to follow it in its vision of the world – those strata that, in the INSEE categories, correspond to the 'intermediary professions' and to certain types of employees in the heart of the urban zones. As we have seen in our analysis of the 2005 referendum, the students

were still strongly pro-European: today they are probably
neo-republican and still identify with the prosperous sectors
of society, to which, however, so many of them will never
belong.

The powerful negative effect of the variable 'proportion
of workers' on the number of demonstrators indicates, on
the other hand, that the lower classes have now completely
escaped from the ideological control of the culturally dominant classes. The geographical organization of society largely
explains this negative liberty. With great realism, Christophe
Guilluy has centred his depiction of French society on the
way the lower classes have been relegated to the periphery.
Forced out into the geographical margins of urban areas, the
workers no longer turn out to demonstrate in the hearts of
town and cities. They can no longer be mobilized on an ad
hoc basis, just as they can no longer be controlled ideologically: witness the way large numbers of them vote for the
National Front. It is true that François Hollande and the
Socialist Party had, by refusing the National Front any place
in the 'great republican demonstrations', implicitly designated NF voters as non-desirables in the heart of our cities.
At a time when the neo-republican pact is being sealed, the
perfectly real category of 'workers' is no more welcome than
the imaginary category of 'Muslims'.

It is a great achievement for the MEZ bloc to have seized
control of the intermediary strata of society, on however
temporary a basis. Remember that the shift from the 51 per
cent 'yes' vote for Maastricht to the 55 per cent 'no' vote for
the Treaty on the European Constitution had resulted from
the defection of these same strata, 57 per cent of which had
voted 'yes' in 1992 but 54 per cent of which had voted 'no'
in 2005. A great achievement, indeed, but one that seems to
open the path to an exploitation of Islamophobia as a means
of social control.

We should avoid overinterpreting the figures: we cannot be certain that the 4 million demonstrators – a figure that is definitely too high – represent more than the 12.7 million who voted 'yes' in 2005 (45 per cent of votes cast). But we should at least admit that the Charlie phenomenon encouraged the collapse of the oppositions within the middle classes, to some extent led to a merging of left and right, and revealed the lack of ideological substance of the left wing of the left.

Secularism versus the left

Many intellectuals and economists on the so-called critical left were caught up in the demand for secularism as a substitute for the critique of free trade and the euro which they are unable to provide. I quoted Christophe Ramaux (above) for his analysis of the social state. On 9 January he was already writing in *Le Monde* to denounce the review *Politis* and the Attac association, both guilty, no doubt, of not indulging in thoughtless Islamophobia. On 11 February, in a new op-ed piece, 'Prolonger l'esprit du 11 janvier du politique à l'économie' ('Extending the spirit of 11 January from the political to the economic sphere'), he discussed public expenditure, but he did not mention leaving the euro or contesting free trade, even though these are the only breaks that would make it possible to implement economic policies favourable to lower-class milieus and young people in urban environments. The defence of the social state of the middle classes is still the absolute priority.

At the start of 2015 there were still, admittedly, many people on the left whose personal doctrine combined, in an unstable mixture, a hostility to Europe and a fear of Islam. But the ideological dynamics within the middle classes has tended to result in the first preoccupation being eliminated by the second.

Thus it was that the vast mass of the left marched behind François Hollande, Nicolas Sarkozy, Angela Merkel, David Cameron, Jean-Claude Juncker, Donald Tusk and Petro Porochenko. As I have said, there is no excuse for ignorance of why you are marching, or at least there is no excuse for not knowing who you are marching behind. What you accept in practice is more significant than what you reject in theory. The main sector of the left wing of the left rejects, in theory and in no particular order: austerity, the capitalist system, American leadership and the oppression suffered by the Palestinians. It accepts, in practice, the single currency and free trade. However, it would be an understatement to say that this pseudo-opposition felt no great compunction about marching behind pro-European leaders. On that fateful day, they accepted that they were part of the MEZ bloc that dominates, ideologically and politically, French society.

Thus, demonstrating in favour of secularism and the right to blasphemy defined a 'partial unanimity', a paradoxical concept but one that is essential for understanding the system that is gradually emerging – a concept that becomes easier to grasp when translated as 'the unanimity of the middle classes'.

These middle classes are under stress due to the pervasive metaphysical void, the failure of the euro and certain effects of neoliberalism. But, far from disintegrating, these same middle classes are bringing about their final ideological and emotional fusion. Socialists, supporters of Sarkozy and supporters of Mélenchon all marched together, affirming the same fundamental values. This sense of unity was authentic and, as it were, therapeutic. Many of them experienced the day of the demonstrations in religious terms, as a unifying new creation of the world, in which they could force out and push down all those depressing second-class citizens who represent ... over half of society. There could be no doubting their sincerity.

Political journalists were temporarily freed from the gravitational field of real life and truly expected that the outcome of 11 January would be the abolition of classes and the conflicts between them. In their fantasy world, the National Front would just evaporate, symbolically destroyed by being excluded from the demonstrations. More reasonably, they also predicted a very short-lived rise in the fortunes of the Socialist Party, led, at last – and this is where their reasonableness came up against its limits – by a real leader, François Hollande.

On the other hand, it is clear that the unification of France's upper echelons that took place on 11 January, combined with the exclusion both of young Muslims from the suburbs and of the workers, emphasized the way society had been 'verticalized' in people's minds. As a result, far from leading to the disappearance of the far right, it opened the floodgates to a new surge in the National Front. Political journalists could have avoided uttering a great deal of nonsense if only they had read the short analysis published on 21 January by Jérôme Fourquet, in which he identified the regional disparities in the number of people demonstrating, the continuing trace of the 'no' vote in the referendum, and the imprint of the National Front in the areas where there were relatively few demonstrators.[1]

On 30 January, the magazine *Marianne* gave Marine Le Pen 30 per cent in the opinion polls. On 8 February, the National Front obtained 48.5 per cent of the vote in the second round of a by-election in the Doubs, behind a socialist

---

[1] IFOP, Focus no. 121, 'Marche républicaine pour Charlie, des disparités de mobilisation lourdes de sens'.

candidate. The (centre-right) UMP (Union pour un mouvement populaire) had been eliminated in the first round.

In the departmental elections in March 2015, the National
Front won a quarter of the vote, and continued to infiltrate
the local level in the context of an abstention rate that fell
back to beneath 50 per cent. The Socialist Party was the
choice of barely more than a fifth of the voters.

Catholicism, Islamophobia and anti-Semitism

Even more than the low representation of workers or the
overrepresentation of the category of 'managerial and
liberal professions', the way the proportion of demonstrators coincided with the old map of Catholicism means we
need to reject the idea of any continuity between traditional
republicanism, with its support for equality, and neo-
republicanism as fashioned by zombie Catholicism. Indeed,
neo-republicanism comes to us from that part of the French
anthropological system that calls for inequality between
people and their social conditions. An examination of their
metaphysical ID will help us understand this doctrine more
deeply and comprehensively. In particular, it will enable us
to put forward a few hypotheses on the relatively small place
Charlie gave to the anti-Semitic dimension of the attacks.
Our aim here is to open up, cautiously, a field for further
research rather than to come to any conclusions.

On 23 January, Marcela Iacub expressed disquiet over this
in *Libération*:

> There was something really rather awkward in the com-
> memoration of the victims of terrorism: the way almost no
> place was given to the Jews who had been killed. People
> will say that in fact they were talked about everywhere,

admittedly rather less than the writers of *Charlie Hebdo* who had died, but they were not completely forgotten. And that's the problem. It is precisely this which leaves a bitter taste in our memories. For there is a feeling that killing people for drawing caricatures of the Prophet is something more serious than killing Jews.

At this point we are coming to the original sin of Charlie. He had been unfazed by the massacres perpetrated in March 2012 by Mohammed Merah, who killed soldiers in Montauban and then a teacher and three Jewish children in the Otzar Hatorah school in Toulouse. And yet there can be no doubt that the killings in Toulouse were morally a whole degree more serious than the killings perpetrated at *Charlie Hebdo*. For it is clear that assassinating children, or adults, simply because they are Jewish, is even more vile than massacring an editorial board that is engaged in a political struggle. In May 2014, Mehdi Nemmouche, a French citizen, had killed four people in the Jewish Museum in Brussels. Problem number one in French society is not the attack on the freedom to draw caricatures, or on the freedom of expression, but the spread of anti-Semitism in its suburbs.

The events of 7 January eventually reproduced, in a minor mode, a general complacency towards anti-Semitism, as the earlier killings had already shown. The demonstrators did not come together primarily to denounce the most serious problem, namely anti-Semitism and the growing danger that one minority religion, Judaism, has to face, but to sacralize the ideological violence inflicted on another minority religion, Islam.

The Charlie phenomenon can be understood only if it is related to the religious sphere – 'religious' here being taken in its broadest sense, which includes the negation of the religious. Militant atheism has its theology: it deems it important, indeed a matter of priority, to affirm the non-existence of God, both the god of its ancestors and the god of others. In the overall religious confusion that character-izes French society, we can note four basic elements:

1 General unbelief.
2 Hostility to Islam, the religion of a dominated group.
3 The rise of anti-Semitism in that dominated group.
4 The relative indifference of the dominant secularized world to the rise of that anti-Semitism.

It is sociologically, politically and humanly clear that, in such a context, *the definition of Islam as the central problem of French society can only lead to an increase in the physical risk, not to the majority of French people, but to Jews.*

Should we view it as a coincidence that the sequence, once set in motion, will go as follows: more militant atheism will lead to more Islamophobia, that will itself lead in turn to more anti-Semitism? Yes, absolutely – if we limit ourselves to the conscious motivations of political and social protagonists. But identifying zombie Catholicism as lying at the heart of the Charlie phenomenon should lead us to be cautious. We cannot just be satisfied with a 'conscious' interpretation of social mechanisms. If we accept the hypothesis of anthropo-logical inertia and the obvious continuity of historical forces, we also need to see, at the heart of Charlie – which defines itself *vis-à-vis* Islam – the lineage of anthropological forces which, to be frank, were not very friendly towards the Jews. France has long been dominated ideologically by universal-ism, but there is also a France which thinks that peoples are different by nature.

A differentialist logic plays an active role in those regions where the anthropological background is inegalitarian. As a psychological mechanism, it can be summed up in a simple sequence: 'If brothers are unequal, peoples are unequal and there is no universal human being. The foreigner, the Jew, the Muslim, the Black, are all by nature different.' This differentialism can be stated in a gentle form, under the heading 'the right to difference', especially in anthropological systems that define brothers as different rather than as frankly unequal. This is the case in Britain and the USA, Holland and Denmark. In general, 'multiculturalism' disguises the sidelining of the targeted group by the use of the expression 'respect for its culture', or the term 'tolerance'. Typically, differentialism is happy to put up with the immigrant, or the Jew, or the Black, or the Muslim, so long as they stay in their place and agree to play the role expected of them: that of being different. It is when they become assimilated and try to become human beings just like everyone else – ordinary citizens – that the non-egalitarian base reacts.

This rejection can be extremely brutal when the underlying family structure is inegalitarian. The limit case of differentialist xenophobia was Nazism, a belated product of the old German family at a time of collapsing religious beliefs and economic crisis. First, it was the assimilated or assimilating Jews who were viewed as intolerable. If the Other is different by nature, its assimilation can only be an illusion, a decoy, a lie, an attempt to inveigle its way into a healthy culture so as to corrupt it from within.

The anti-Semitism that manifested itself in France at the time of the Dreyfus Affair was a moderate variant of the differentialist type. It was rooted in the Catholic part of the French bourgeoisie and on its periphery, against an inegalitarian anthropological backdrop. However, the populations concerned were imbued with a living and healthy Catholicism and were not undergoing any religious crisis. In fact, this Catholicism was itself a moderating influence as, by tradition, it bore a universal message. It fully acknowledged that it was a descendant, by legitimate lineage, of Judaism. But it was assimilated Jews, the French 'Israelites' of the end of the nineteenth century, who were targeted.

The protection guaranteed by the dominant egalitarian culture, which on principle refused to see human beings – including assimilated Jews – as different, ensured that the Dreyfusards won.

In the case of egalitarian anthropological systems, as we have seen, the sequence is reversed: 'Brothers are equal, human beings are equal, peoples are equal and there is a universal human being.'

Clearly, any resistance, any slowness in the process of assimilation aroused exasperation in an egalitarian host society that operated on the basis of a universalist prejudice. In a spirit of impartiality, I will show, in Chapter 4 (where I discuss the French on the far right), that there can be a xenophobia that is universalist in essence and, at certain times of crisis, an authentically republican anti-Semitism. This rarer form derives from an exaggerated application of the principle of equality, which follows an opposite logic from Catholic or Vichyist anti-Semitism: the latter comes, traditionally, from a routine application of the principle of inequality. At this stage of our analysis, we will simply note one fundamental if partial fact. In a France that has just come under the control of its zombie Catholic periphery, an obsessional religious climate is developing with a set of resentments fitted into one another like so many Russian dolls: Islamophobia in the population of Christian origin, and anti-Semitism in the population of Muslim origin.

We need to fill out our analysis of the ideological shift that is currently disorientating French society. If we are to understand the rise of the value of inequality, we need more fully to take the measure of the malaise affecting *la France centrale*, the France that is secular and egalitarian. Even more than the dynamism proper to zombie Catholicism, it is the implosion of this *France centrale* that explains the emergence of the neo-republican system. More than the strength of Vichy, it is the weakness of the Revolution that explains why the Republic has become distorted. For the value of equality is in poor shape, in France, in Europe, and, if truth be told, throughout the developed world.

3

When Equality Fails

As Thomas Piketty and his colleagues have shown, the crisis in equality is a worldwide phenomenon. It would be unrealistic to seek an explanation for it in a purely French context. The concentration of capital, the rising inequalities in income and the emergence of oligarchies are global phenomena. The neoliberal organization of business and finance has allowed them to emerge, but does not explain them. It is states that have drawn up the rules of the game which have led to an increase in inequalities. It is *representative political systems* that have accepted and organized the widening of the range of incomes. Nothing of this has been unplanned. The most orthodox economic theory – from Ricardo's comparative advantages to the theorem of Heckscher-Ohlin – predicted that inequality would accompany efficiency. I am happy to admit that the elite *énarques*,[1] who, in France,

---

[1] Graduates of the École nationale d'administration, or ENA. (Translator's note.)

govern the major banks and the state, had not anticipated the drop in median income that we are witnessing today. But at the same time as electoral bodies adopted the new status quo, they also acclaimed the discourse hailing the triumph of individualism, the neoliberal rules of the game, the need for competition, and the promised benefits of inequality.

So what we still need to identify is the factor, common to all advanced societies, that will explain this mass allegiance to the new order. We should immediately rule out the conspiracy theory which deems that it is highly placed sects that are manipulating public opinion and the media. To grasp how the body of the citizens has been dissolved, we will instead observe how the educational level in different populations has developed.

Around 1945, at the dawn of the *Trente Glorieuses*,[1] everyone, or almost everyone, could read and write, in Europe and Japan if not always elsewhere. In the United States, 80 per cent of young people had by this date received a secondary school education. In the most developed countries as a whole, the implicit dominant trend was democratic. The level of cultural competence varied little from one class to another. Politicians, ideologues and novelists who had benefited from a higher education needed, if they wanted to exist socially, to 'speak' to the masses. However, the development of higher education made any educational homogeneity more fragile: this homogeneity was broken and dislocated everywhere, from the 1950s onwards in the United States, and from the 1970s and 1980s in Europe and Japan.

The cultural pyramid is turned upwards down when it comes to the younger generations. These are tending towards a new stratification, with, on a very schematic

[1] The 'Thirty Glorious Years' (1945–75) refers to the post-war boom in France. (Translator's note.)

model, 45 per cent having had a short or long tertiary education, 45 per cent a complete secondary education, and 10 per cent little education beyond primary school level. In this upside-down cultural pyramid, primary education can hardly be described as anything other than failure in education. When official statistics target the educationally unprivileged, they keep slipping from the concept of 'primary education alone' to 'leaving the educational system without any qualifications' – or, even more explicitly, 'difficulties in reading'. Having been a pillar of democracy, mass literacy has become the synonym of inadequacy, a symbol of failure. The egalitarian feelings that were infused in people by universal primary education have been succeeded by feelings of social inegalitarianism. True, these feelings are not the same for everybody. The happy consciousness of belonging to the elite category of those with a higher education is echoed either by the unhappy consciousness of the inferior category of primary education, or by the uncertain consciousness of the intermediate strata of the secondary system. This is the origin of the confrontation between elitism and populism that is found in all major Western democracies. The split is less evident in Germany, Japan, Switzerland and Sweden: in all these countries, societies are protected from the most devastating effects of the new inegalitarian subconscious, thanks to their vertical integration.

But the new cultural stratification is, of course, the main cause behind the vote for the National Front. Here, educational factors play an even more important role than economic factors. However, we cannot consider the National Front as primary or, as it were, 'elementary'. It is those who have benefited from a 'secondary' education that form the majority of its ranks. Those with a 'higher' education behind them are, as yet, immune to its charms. In very schematic terms, the younger part of the population that is likely to join the National Front comes from: primary (10 per cent) + secondary (45 per cent) = 55 per cent of the population. This calculation does not take into the account the way in which the numbers of the far right will inevitably be swollen by those who have received a higher education, but whose incomes – already low, given their qualifications – have shrunk sufficiently.

The difficulties of secular, egalitarian France

France's anthropological diversity makes this country an extraordinary laboratory for anyone seeking to understand not just the universality of the trend towards inequality, but also the diversity of its effects on society. The rise in the value of inequality does not have the same implications when the anthropological base is inegalitarian and accepts it on principle, and when this same base is egalitarian and suffers, resists and rejects the general tendency.

So how do the two Frances – the France of inequality and the France of equality – react?

Working on the data from the most recent censuses, Hervé Le Bras and I observed, in our book *Le Mystère français*, how Catholicism had survived its own death in the peripheral regions – an observation which, as I have said, made it necessary to introduce the concept of 'zombie Catholicism' into our models. Several statistical indicators showed that something, in regions indifferent or hostile to equality, was still at work, finding expression in better results at school, fewer family problems, lower unemployment rates and more successful economic redeployment. Symmetrically, the old egalitarian and secular France was not in the best of health. The map for unemployment in 2014 (3.2) shows a positive correlation, not a big one but highly significant, with residual religious practice, in other words with zombie Catholicism (–0.30).

The difference in educational performance is certainly the general driving force behind the better performances among zombie Catholics and the difficulties of the secular parts of the country. What is most surprising here is probably the higher degree of educational polarization observed in the regions of an egalitarian temperament: what we find here, relatively speaking, is a great number of those educated in primary school *and* a great number of those with a higher education.

In tandem with the results that we presented in *Le Mystère français*, other researchers have worked on identifying the regions that are in educational difficulties. Our conclusions converge. Map 3.1 shows us the result of a very detailed analysis that, for the academic year 2001–2, identifies those *départements* that *scored too highly* in the national assessment test for children in year seven, and those that *scored exceptionally poorly* once the predictable factors of socioeconomic milieu, family problems and the proportion of foreigners have been eliminated.[1] What we then see is two major poles suffering from difficulties: yet again they are the two hearts of de-Christianized France, namely the central Paris Basin and Provence.

When we discovered this, we were initially aware of the positive face of the phenomenon: the higher rate of success in traditionally Catholic regions. Their performance could, in a first analysis, be explained by two factors that complemented each other. The first will doubtless be music to Christian ears: the survival of social disciplines stemming from the

---

[1] Sylvain Broccolichi, Choukri Ben-Aye, Catherine Mathey-Pierre and Danièle Trancart, 'Fragmentations territoriales et inégalités scolaires: des relations complexes entre la distribution spatiale, les conditions de scolarisation et la réussite des élèves', *Éducation & formations* no. 74, April 2007.

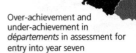

Over-achievement and
under-achievement in
départements in assessment for
entry into year seven

■ 3 and more
■ from 2 to 2.9
■ from 1 to 1.9
■ from −1 to 0.9
▨ from −1.1 to −2
▨ from −2.1 to −4
▨ below −4

(Plus or minus value depending
on social structure)

Map 3.1   Educational difficulties

teachings of the Church – family stability, local cooperation, an anti-individualist morality: these all constitute protective layers in a neocapitalist society being undermined by the isolation of individuals, egotism or, worse, mass narcissism, not to mention the ideology which deems that all work that

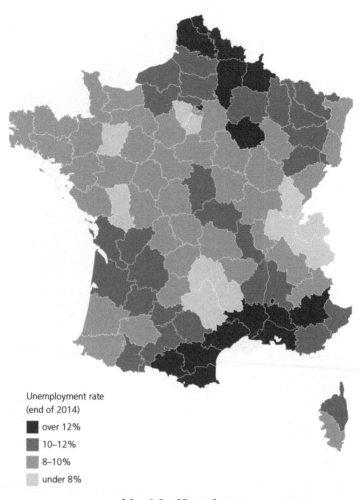

Unemployment rate
(end of 2014)

■ over 12%

■ 10–12%

■ 8–10%

□ under 8%

Map 3.2   Unemployment

does not instantly lead to profit is on principle seen as of less worth. Two thinkers from Central Europe, aware of the anthropological and cultural origins of the Nazi disaster, had a better understanding than did many others of the importance of protective social layers in people's ability to resist the reductive abstractions of the market place. Admittedly, the vision of Joseph Schumpeter, as he set it out in 1942, was still quite elitist, as he still thought that most of the protections that had come down from the past were located at the top of the social structure, among those civilized and benevolent aristocracies.[1] But in 1944, Karl Polanyi managed to place the emergence of capitalism within its anthropological context and to understand the threat that the erosion of protective levels by the market posed for human life. Here is what he says:

> To allow the market mechanism to be sole director of the fate of human beings and their natural environment, indeed, even of the amount and use of purchasing power, would result in the demolition of society. For the alleged commodity 'labor power' cannot be shoved about, used indiscriminately, or even left unused, without affecting also the human individual who happens to be the bearer of this particular commodity. In disposing of a man's labor power the system would, incidentally, dispose of the physical, psychological, and moral entity 'man' attached to that tag. Robbed of the protective covering of human institutions, human beings would perish from the effects of social exposure; they would die as the victims of acute social dislocation through vice, perversion, crime, and starvation.[2]

Reading Polanyi, it is clear how the habit of supervising individuals via what is left of the Catholic practices of cooperation and mutual aid has managed to protect, over the last thirty years, a third of French regions – practices that

---

[1] Joseph Schumpeter, *Capitalism, Socialism and Democracy* (London: Routledge, 2010).
[2] Karl Polanyi, *The Great Transformation* (Boston, MA: Beacon Press, 1957), p. 76.

are cruelly lacking in *la France centrale*, with its individualist egalitarianism.

The second factor that explains the success of zombie Catholicism is less favourable to the Church, and lies rather within the secular or Protestant tradition. Rome, that obscurantist monster, tried to stem progress and education, encouraging universal submission to the priest. So it is only to be expected that the collapse of the clerical control of consciences should have freed people's energies and led to a sense of optimism. In fact, we can imagine, in the eighteenth-century Paris Basin and Provence, how a similar phenomenon took place. Diderot came from the Haute-Marne, Condorcet from the Aisne, Robespierre from the Pas-de-Calais, and Saint-Just from the Nièvre. Between 1819 and 1826, the *départements* of the Paris Basin sent a disproportionate number of students to the major Paris elite schools, especially along the Somme/Haute-Marne axis.[1] The nation's egalitarian heart, especially in its northeastern part, was beating loud and clear both on the eve of, and in the immediate aftermath of, the French Revolution. Or, more precisely, it was electrifying every aspect of life: culturally ahead of the rest of the country, it was producing more innovative elites and creating a higher suicide level. The decline of religion means both hope and turmoil.

In the zombie Catholic provinces, hope certainly won out over turmoil between 1960 and 1990, especially in a western France that had just discovered not just the consumer society, but all the accumulated forms of modernity, including a belated and sophisticated industrial revolution. The economic dynamism of the Choletais and Mayenne areas was a result of this new state of mind.

---

[1] Hervé Le Bras and Emmanuel Todd, *L'Invention de la France*, new edn (Paris: Gallimard, 2012), p. 269.

We should not fail to notice, however, that part of the success of these regions, especially since 1990, is the result neither of their traditions of mutual aid, nor of their liberation from the grip of the priests, but quite simply from the fact that, in their depths, in a worldwide historical phase in which inequalities are increasing, they accept this inequality as a matter of course. Their active populations are more docile than those that live in the egalitarian *France centrale*. There is a twofold advantage to this docility. On the one hand, social tranquillity facilitates, internally, the smooth functioning of the regional economic mechanism; on the other, such a society, well disposed towards managers, draws in investment from outside. You do not need to be an anthropologist or a historian to perceive the social discipline predominant in zombie Catholic societies: the CFDT majority there advocates intelligent cooperation, which in times of economic difficulty when wages are falling may remind us of the forelock-tugging gratitude shown to superiors in the old feudal societies of western France.

Admittedly, things are more complicated in the east of France, where industry has long been established, but managers from Lyons, Alsace and Savoie know that they can always count on workers who are less keen on the value of equality than elsewhere. The anthropology of family structures here merely makes explicit what everyone already knows. In the current phase of capitalism, the accelerated mobility of capital favours, both inside nations and on the global scale, societies that can cope most easily with inequality.

The difficulties of secular regions can, in symmetric fashion, be explained by the inversion of all the positive factors that we have just enumerated for the Catholic zombie regions. Their egalitarian individualism leaves men and women without any safety net in a period of rapid social evolution and never-ending economic redeployment. In these parts, de-Christianization was accomplished long ago and has lost its optimistic message of liberation.

One supplementary factor of turmoil can be added to the ones we have already noted in the France of equality. The evaporation of communism has left the lower-class world orphaned by the great Red Church; furthermore, this world is expected to feel ashamed of the support it showed for communism for over half a century. The French ideologues of 1990–2010, feverishly busy denouncing – usually after the battle had already been won – the misdemeanours of a now-vanquished communism, neglected to notice what their country had lost with the decline of the French Communist Party. What had gone was a huge cultural machine that, in the secular two-thirds of France, in lower-class milieus, had kept alive the faith in progress and education, in other words the best aspects of bourgeois culture, not forgetting its trust in the universal and its rejection of xenophobia. Stalinist in its administrative practices, the French Communist Party was liberal in its values and elevated in its morality. It would not accept activists who made anti-Arab remarks. I am here drawing on my own memories of the party in the years between 1967 and 1969. The decline of *la France centrale* and its current pessimism partly result from the collapse of the Communist Party.

And the negative implications are twofold. Capital has no love for those regions of social indiscipline and class conflict. It has long been the case that people are reluctant to invest in zones dominated by the CGT, whose geography is just as surely dominated by a longstanding secularism as that of the CFDT is by religious practice. Secular France is in a bad shape, not just because its endogenous dynamism is less, but also because capital punishes it, day after day, for its prefer- ence for equality, its rejection of social deference. In its case, there is a latent 'no God, no master' mentality.

Without this crisis in *la France centrale*, the opposite values of the periphery would never have won out. In terms of territory, the France of inequality is no more significant than it used to be, but its anthropological base is well adapted to the current movement of history, whose main axis is the rush towards inequality. The new educational stratification confirms the ideological principles at work in inegalitarian zones based on family and religion. But this still leaves one question: in this process, what happens to the values of the middle classes that emerged from egalitarian zones, those strata that have been greatly enlarged by the development of higher education? Have they been transformed in depth? Might the group of managerial and liberal professions, which still comprises between a fifth and a third of the active population in the egalitarian urban zone, escaped from its anthropological matrix? This question already concerns Paris, of course. Should we consider the egalitarianism of the Île-de-France as destroyed, or just temporarily deactivated? I will return to this delicate point once I have examined the mode of reproduction of the anthropological systems involved.

Meanwhile, we should note that these conclusions, reached for France, are valid throughout the developed world, where it is the nations with an egalitarian temperament that are in difficulty.

The anthropology of a capitalism in crisis

At the risk of aggravating French anxiety, we need to admit first and foremost that the precocious development of capitalism was brought about by nations whose anthropological basis, if not inegalitarian, was at least not egalitarian. This is true of the Anglo-American world as a whole, which provided global capitalism with its two successive leaders, Great

Britain in the nineteenth century and the United States in the twentieth. The absolute nuclear family combines, in these two countries, a liberalism in relations between parents and children with the absence of any principle of equality in the relations between brothers and sisters. From the anthropological point of view, Denmark and Holland (but not the Low Countries as a whole) are quite close to the Anglo-American world, just like inland western France, under its Catholic veneer.

The second wave of economic take-offs occurred in countries where the stem family predominated – Germany, Sweden, Japan and Korea – and where inequality and authority were frankly encouraged by the family structure. One heir, usually the oldest boy, succeeded to the farm. The Swedish variant was an interesting feminist deviation of a model still young and very imperfect there in the nineteenth century.

The dominant economic powers of the Western world are thus, from the anthropological point of view, a world without any egalitarian substratum.[1] It is immediately apparent how the acceptance of a difference in principle between brothers, between human beings and between classes encouraged the functional differentiation of the nascent industrial world.

This 'Western' world, however, is not ideologically homogeneous. The authoritarianism of the stem family contrasts with the liberalism of the absolute nuclear family. The frank inegalitarianism of Germany and Japan is not the same as the tolerance of inequality found in the Anglo-American world. Without this contrast, the choices made by these different countries in the Second World War would be impossible to

---

[1] For a recent statistical and econometric verification of this thesis, see David le Bris, 'Family characteristics and economic development', Kedge Business School, 2015.

understand. The Nazi notion of the absolute inequality of human beings who are the prisoners of their race is inconceivable for Anglo-American liberals, who simply feel that human beings are not really equal between themselves.

The Europe of inequality

The Europe of inequality, and not just *la France centrale*, is in difficulties. Italy, Spain and Portugal had already fallen behind by the start of the twentieth century; now, in the twenty-first century, they are being robbed blind by Northern Europe. The exceptions are on a smaller scale: Finland, for instance, which in its non-Swedish part is egalitarian, and where there was until very recently a significant Communist Party, is in pretty good shape. Its Lutheran religion, imposed in the sixteenth century by the Swedes, has enabled it to temper the egalitarianism of its family life with the inequality of predestination. Greece is another exception: its continental area, particularly in the mass of the country to the north of the Gulf of Corinth, is egalitarian, but the highly unusual anthropological tradition on the islands rests on a family system based on feminine primogeniture. Be this as it may, Greece, enslaved by Northern Europe, cannot be considered as viscerally egalitarian.

The fact remains that, essentially speaking, the hierarchical ordering of Europe, under German leadership, is following a clear anthropological logic. The inegalitarian North, whether Protestant or not, is resuming its historical precedence over the egalitarian South.

The hierarchical ordering of the continent echoes the dislocation of France. In Europe, the Germanic and inegalitarian heart, economically dominant, is assuming control of the egalitarian periphery. In France, the egalitarian heart, suffering from an economic slow-down, is losing control of its inegalitarian periphery. We might even say that the centre is coming under the control of the periphery, with the zombie Catholic regions relying on European mechanisms to keep a grip on the country as a whole. To simplify matters, let's start out from what is now the central power in Europe, Germany: the zombie Catholic provinces play the role of a mediator between the German system and French territory.

If we look at Europe as a whole, we see a continent-wide zombie Catholicism combined with family values. The dynamism of Flanders, the Veneto and Italy northeast of the Po, Ireland, Austria and Poland results from the fall of religious practice in regions that used to be among the Church's strongest bastions. In Germany itself, Bavaria and Baden-Württemberg, with their Catholic majorities, show higher rates of growth than the Protestant north. The redeployment of the Ruhr has, however, put a brake on the rise of the Catholic Rhineland. Slovenia and Croatia could, if they succeed in adapting to changed economic circumstances, join the Catholic zombie group. The variety of underlying family structures in these regions does not prevent them sharing a common characteristic: the absence of the principle of equality.

Thus there is, in Europe as a whole as in France, a constellation of inegalitarian zombie Catholic regions, a large majority of which are in the Eurozone. Insofar as this anthropo-religious type is the only one really shared by several nations, we can venture the hypothesis that it comprises the real backbone of the single currency. There is nothing extraordinary in this suggestion, which merely adds recent de-Christianization to the traditional view that European construction is the daughter of Christian democracy. Emptied of its belief in God, Catholic culture invented the euro. Freed of the obligations of compassion and charity, its hierarchical conception of social life is becoming stronger and harsher. Day after day, this inegalitarian ideal is organizing a little more tightly the inner lives of societies and the relations between the different European peoples.

France, the Germans and the Arabs

In the case of France, nothing shows the inversion of the dominant ideology more clearly than the development of the country's relation with the two peoples who, in the twentieth century, caused it problems: the Germans and the Arabs. Under de Gaulle, the dominant ideal was one of equality between nations and peoples. The rule was applied irrespective of a sense of inferiority *vis-à-vis* a militarily and economically victorious Germany and a sense of superiority *vis-à-vis* the Arab world, i.e. France's colonies. General de Gaulle's policies towards Germans and Arabs were, in spirit, both universalist. This ideological principle gradually and imperceptibly changed until the current hierarchical order was produced. Germany is redefined as superior and has to be imitated or obeyed. The Arab world is perceived as inferior and has to be modernized or marginalized. These two movements are in fact one and the same, an element in the inegalitarian reorganization of the mental system of the ruling elite. It is part of a 'Vichyist' rather than a 'republican' tradition.

This tendency is at loggerheads with another, more egalitarian trend, which consists in hating all peoples equally: this might be called 'universalist xenophobia', in virtue of which you can be a Germanophobe, an Islamophobe and a Russophobe all at the same time. I will try to explain later on what these two competing xenophobias, the one egalitarian and the other hierarchizing, mean, and what causes them.

At the present stage, in France, these xenophobias either cosy up to or avoid one another, in a diabolical dance. The elite is almost entirely Russophobe. The Socialist Party, officially, loves everybody except the Russians. The UMP is European and Islamophobic, but less strict in its Russophobia. The National Front is Europhobic, Islamophobic – but Russophile.

Inherent developments within Germany and Northern European countries are starting to produce a new order. Islamophobia increasingly seems to be Europe's horizon, and French political parties will be faced with a choice. Michel Houellebecq's *Submission* was a bestseller, not just in France but also in Italy and Germany. We should at all costs refrain here from imagining that Paris is the capital city of new ideas. Our commercial balance is, in the Islamophobic area as in so many others, clearly in the red.

Germany and circumcision

All the classic elements of Islamophobia are present in Germany, to a high degree. They include certain bestsellers 'made in Germany' such as *Germany is Doing Away with Itself*, published in 2010: it has sold more than two million copies. Its author, Thilo Sarrazin, is a Social Democratic politician, born in the heart of Protestant Germany, in Gera, Thuringia. His book caused a scandal, and its publication meant that Sarrazin had to resign from his post on the executive board of the Bundesbank. The original German title of the book, *Deutschland schafft sich ab*, is well captured by the title of the English translation: it also means 'Germany is abolishing itself', and we are forced to admit that Éric Zemmour, with his *Suicide français* of 2014, is just a modest epigone of an ideological evolution whose centre of gravity lies more to the east and to the north. Likewise, when *Charlie Hebdo* started systematically to make fun of Muhammad, this satirical magazine was just an epigone of the Danish daily newspaper *Jyllands-Posten*, which had 'launched the debate' in 2005 by publishing several caricatures relating to Islam. The one that drew the widest attention was by the Danish cartoonist Kurt Westergaard, showing Muhammad wearing a turban in the shape of a bomb. Though it was instinctually in solidarity with the ideologues of the North, *Charlie Hebdo* was to some extent just an imitator. Yet again, it is Protestant Europe that is setting the pace, although the proportion of Muslims in its population is much lower than in France or in the Catholic part of Germany.

Let's go back a bit further in time: to the murder, on 6 May 2002, of Pim Fortuyn, the leader of a Dutch Islamophobic party, preceding the *Charlie Hebdo* killings by thirteen years. In the Netherlands, it sparked a national outcry at least as great as that of 7 January 2015 in France. Fortuyn came from the Socialist Party and from northern, i.e. Protestant, Holland.

In 2014, in Germany, the political organization Pegida was founded: the name stands for 'Patriotische Europäer gegen die Islamisierung des Abendlandes' or, in English, 'Patriotic Europeans against the Islamization of the West', though this translation loses the twilit nuance of the term *Abendlandes* (evening land, or the land of the setting sun). A crisis in the movement's internal growth seems to have curbed the enthusiasm behind its Monday evenings in Dresden – so this too is a phenomenon of the Protestant part of the country.

When we are looking for cutting-edge Islamophobia, however, there are more interesting things going on in Germany than the murky nocturnal gatherings of the Pegida organization: the unconscious of the judicial elites and ordinary folk, an unconscious that shows how easy it is for Islamophobia to converge with anti-Semitism.

At the end of 2010, the circumcision of a 4-year-old Tunisian boy led to bleeding: this was treated at the hospital. A prosecutor brought a case against the doctor, a Syrian, for 'grievous bodily harm with aggravating factors'. A first court threw the case out. The prosecutor, a man of some persistence, went to the appeal courts, which discharged the doctor but decided on 7 May 2012 that circumcision was a crime, as it modifies the body in a 'permanent and irreparable way'. So circumcision, a Jewish, Muslim and widespread American tradition (about half of American males are circumcised) was defined by a German court as an irreversible mutilation because 'the right of a child to its physical integrity is more important than the parents' right'. In Germany, this decision led to a hilariously po-faced debate at the end of which opinion polls revealed that 55 per cent of Germans approved of the decision. Protests from Israel finally brought Angela Merkel and the German political parties back down to the world as it actually is, and a bill authorizing religious minorities to practise circumcision was passed in the Bundestag on 12 December 2012, by 434 votes to 100, with 46 abstentions. But that was not the end of the German saga of circumcision.

At the end of September 2013, the Social Democratic Member of Parliament Marlene Rupprecht put forward a resolution to the Parliamentary Assembly of the Council of Europe inviting member states to take measures against 'violation of the physical integrity of children'. It was passed, with 78 votes for, 13 against and 15 abstentions. Members of the European Parliament requested that states 'publicly condemn the most harmful practices, such as female genital mutilation, and pass legislation banning these', and 'clearly define the medical, sanitary and other conditions to be ensured for practices which are today widely carried out in certain religious communities, such as the non-medically justified circumcision of young boys'. Rupprecht had long been a Member of Parliament for a constituency near Nuremberg, in the part of Bavaria where there is a Protestant minority.

Yet again, the State of Israel was forced to react to this proposal, which ordinary common sense ought to have suggested was anti-Semitic and Islamophobic, though it was impossible to say which of the two religions was being targeted most. Rupprecht sees herself as someone engaged in the fight for children's rights. But it is Germany's obsession with circumcision that is really fascinating. In their fieldwork, anthropologists never define it as a problem, least of all for the child. Surveys show that the circumcised and uncircumcised are both equally delighted to be the way they are. So it is quite simply stupefying to see Germany setting itself up, less than seventy years after exterminating a million Jewish children, as a judge of the physical integrity of other Jewish children on its territory, *in all good conscience*. Of course, in Germany there is a feeling that you conform to the modern logic of the child's well-being. The absence of any critical distance from oneself, which is the precondition for a minimal sense of humour, would suffice to characterize the Germans – collectively, not individually, of course – as a people apart, not naturally anti-Semitic or Islamophobic, to be sure, but at least schizoid. And the same schizoid mental structure is at work in the policy of austerity that Germany, with the support of neo-republican France, has imposed on Southern Europe.

The silence of European political parties, which supposedly wallow in the cult of the Shoah, is revealing – but it is not easy to say quite *what* it reveals. Two interpretations are possible. The first would insist on the moral flabbiness of European elites. This would be a reassuring hypothesis.

The second would point to a tacit acquiescing, an approval of the new German problematics of circumcision, and this is a much more disquieting hypothesis – albeit one towards which the positive vote for the European resolution steers us. Though we cannot at this stage reach any firm conclusion, we have to admit that a sincere attachment to the fight against anti-Semitism, on the part of the rulers of the continent, is no longer certain.

The historians of the future will have the job of tracing the genealogy of the new and renewed forms of xenophobia that are gradually invading the European dream at the beginning of the third millennium. However, it is already apparent that the Europe of the Lutheran tradition, which practises its religion just as little as does the Catholic part of the continent, plays a particular role as a catalyst for Islamophobia. I noted above the existence of a zombie Catholic backbone in the Eurozone, with its bastions in Bavaria, Baden, Württemberg, the Rhineland, Austria, the southern Netherlands, Flanders, Ireland, northern Italy, northwest Spain and the periphery of France. The existence of a non-egalitarian anthropological background common to these regions forms the main basis for the emergence of inegalitarianism in the Eurozone. So we now need to add to our model a second constellation, this time zombie Protestant in character, more to the north: it is just as inegalitarian but more active in its adoption of Islamophobic ideas. In the case of Lutheran Germany, we should add that this is just as it had been during the rise of anti-Semitism. In the post-mortem survival of zombie Protestantism, we can sense a surfeit of inegalitarianism stemming from the dogma of predestination. The two constellations, zombie Catholic and zombie Protestant, mix together and complete one another in the Netherlands and Germany.

The great pro-European happening of 11 January 2015

The heads of state who marched at the front of the demonstration were staging a display of the Europe of inequality. I will leave to one side the case of Benjamin Netanyahu, the head of the Israeli executive, whose presence was justified by other preoccupations, such as the risks now hovering over practising Jews in France; I will also leave the case of Serge Lavrov until later.

The whole Almanach de Gotha of postmodern inequality was there in force: Angela Merkel (domination, austerity), François Hollande (obedience), David Cameron (neoliberalism), Anne Hidalgo (the managerial and liberal professions of Paris), Jean-Claude Juncker (the Luxembourg banking system), Nicolas Sarkozy (the first wave of Islamophobia in France), Donald Tusk (Russophobia), etc.

We should thank François Hollande for his sincerity. Worn down for months on end by massively negative opinion polls, and unsettled, on 7 January, by the sudden return of tragedy to the history of France, he allowed his unconscious to speak and presented us with an authentic coming out of inegalitarianism. I can imagine what a weight it was off his mind, after all the sufferings that he must have endured after the recitation of his egalitarian speech at Le Bourget, where he stated: 'My true enemy has no name, no face, no party. He will never stand for election. And yet he holds power. My enemy is the world of finance.' Was this actually what he had said? But where on earth had he got that idea from – that the world of finance had no face and would never be elected? The fact remains that, his hand forced by the terrorist horror, Hollande finally told us the truth about himself and about the French republic. In the invitations he issued, he gave us his own personal definition of Charlie.

I have to confess that, ever the completest, I was for a while worried by the absence of Jérôme Cahuzac (tax dodging). You think I'm exaggerating? Front pages and magazine covers of the time, uniformly imbued with the 'I am Charlie' spirit, suggested this possibility: *Gala* was Charlie, *Closer* was Charlie, I can't remember which porn mag was Charlie, *Mickey* was Charlie. So why not have Cahuzac marching shoulder to shoulder with Juncker, the tax dodger next to his tax haven in person? Cahuzac too, a Socialist minister who held a secret foreign bank account and was forced to resign, embodies one of the true 'values' of the French Republic.

So it seems that a throng of between 1.5 and 2 million people agreed to march behind this incredible collection of monetary, budgetary and military geeks. Domination is accepted; inequality has a mass base. The French Republic, like the European Republic of which it is part, is a hierarchical system. This huge neo-republican demonstration forces us to admit that the rise of inequality in France is not the result of a conspiracy of a tiny elite, or even of the 1 per cent of people with the highest incomes. A demonstration on the part of these people would *by definition* (and even if 100 per cent of them had demonstrated, excluding the over-75s and under-5s) not have brought together more than 500,000 people from the whole of France. Yes, France is indeed mutating into an oligarchical system, but it would be wrong to see at its head, as in bygone days, a very exclusive club of 200 families, or even of 150,000 people. There is a mass oligarchy emerging, defined by a higher educational level and acceptable incomes. It has the country in its grip, imposes its values and its dreams upon it, forces the children of immigrants out into the suburbs, and the French lower classes into the more distant suburbs and the far-flung *départements*.

Russia: an exceptional case

The group of politicians, like the throng of the demonstrators, contained accidental elements of its own, people who were there for other reasons and in virtue of other logics, cut off from the main flow of events. Serge Lavrov, representing Russia, and invisible to the TV cameras, was one of these. He was relegated to the margins: this was all part of a finely orchestrated production, as is the Western aggression that, day by day, Russia is now forced to suffer. Russophobia, just like Islamophobia, has a meaning.

By nature, anthropology resists the blah-blah of ideology. It discerns the reality of national and regional values under politicians' flights of well-meaning fancy. It provides us with an access to the unconscious of peoples and their leaders. I have just referred to the long-term predominance of inegalitarian family values in the Germanic world, non-egalitarian values in England, and the recent rise of the inequality of peripheral regions in France. Russian family values, meanwhile, are strongly egalitarian. The Russian family was communitarian and exogamous in type. It brought a father and his married sons together in huge communities where life and work were shared. It had the peculiar feature of maintaining women in a relatively high status thanks to the recent character of its patrilineal organization, which first arose in the seventeenth century. The Russian tradition combined a strong authoritarianism in relations between parents and children with a strict equality in relations between brothers. It meant oppression among the peasants and intimacy among the nobility. It gave us not only communism and Dostoevsky, but Tolstoy and Turgenev too. Russia, in fact, is the fourth element in the game of European families. *La France centrale* combines liberty with equality; England combines liberty with the absence of equality; Germany combines authority with inequality. Russia joins equality with authority.

The Russian family, which exploded in the second half of the nineteenth century, spread its values of authority and equality through social life as a whole. When these values reached the ideological sphere, they produced Bolshevism, the single party, the planned economy and the KGB. Over time, and following the development of higher education, the violent form of Russian communitarianism faded away. The collapse of the Soviet system, after a period of hesitancy and doubt, favoured the emergence of a market economy guided by the state. After the fall of communism, family values, hidden but permanent, preserved an authoritarian and egalitarian sensibility in Russia. And the persistence of these values is turning Russia, perhaps contrary to its own apparent desires, into a kind of bulwark of resistance to the expansion of Western neoliberalism.

Authoritarianism is driving Russia away from France – this is definitely true, just as the authoritarianism of Germany will before long dissociate it from its French partner. But the France of Charles de Gaulle would have immediately perceived in Vladimir Putin's Russia a sister power, also egalitarian and like France able to sustain the vision of a world of equal nations. Russia remains weakly liberal at home, but its egalitarian perception of human fraternity within and between peoples points to its role as worldwide defender of the Gaullist concept of 'free and equal nations'.

The French neo-republic of François Hollande, where the value of equality has just lost power, cannot possibly love Putin's Russia. Because of the hatred that Western elites feel for Moscow, Lavrov's marginalization to the outer edges of the neo-republican march was only logical.

The mystery of Paris

The presence at the head of the demonstration of Anne Hidalgo, the Mayor of Paris, enables us to bring this chapter to a close by raising one fundamental issue. Paris, after all, plays a major role in the inegalitarian drift of the national system, though we cannot locate the primary cause for this phenomenon within its latent anthropological system.

Paris is at the heart of those regions that have an egalitarian nuclear family. Until the eighteenth century, most of its populace came from that central area, bringing into the nation's very heart the values of a liberal and egalitarian family system. In the nineteenth and then the twentieth century, immigration from the periphery of France became more significant, as did immigration from the rest of Europe and then the whole world. The existence, until very recently, of a red belt dominated by the Communist Party shows that the egalitarianism of the Paris region had not been diminished by the migrations of the nineteenth century and the first half of the twentieth.

The big provincial cities continue to operate essentially the same way as Paris had done in the eighteenth century, drawing the bulk of their population from regional hinterlands, including along the Rhine/Rhône axis, where there is a significant degree of immigration from distant origins. As we have seen, this is how Rennes and Lyons persist as Catholic zombie entities, and Marseilles continues to rejoice in being Marseilles, in all its magical unruliness.

As for Paris, it is turning into what we might call a world-city, in which all the peoples on earth can be found. What we know about the mechanisms of assimilation in the cities of the United States, a country that preceded France in the universalization of the process of migration, suggests that it would be wrong to imagine that there has been a dissolution of the original anthropological system of the host country. In New York, Boston, Chicago, San Francisco and Los Angeles, the family can always be described as an absolute nuclear family. The liberal but non-egalitarian values of the initial English matrix have emerged intact from three centuries of immigration – Scottish, Irish, German, Swedish, Polish, Jewish, Italian, Japanese, Korean and Chinese. By the second or third generation, the descendants of immigrants, whatever their original family system, adopt the system of the host country.

The memory of places

The historical lesson of American anthropology is of great significance for anthropology. *It relativizes the supposed force of the values fostered by the family*, and it takes us away from a 'psychoanalytical' model that imagines it is only *strong values* that are transmitted, as if nailed into the unconscious of children with great hammer blows. Such mechanisms do exist, no doubt, but we also have to accept that *weak values* are transmitted too, reproduced by an environment that extends beyond the family and includes the school, the street, the district and the business, in accordance with a diffuse and gentle mimetic process. The territory transmits its values just as much as does the family. Without this hypothesis, we would not be able to understand the existence of the United States, Canada or Australia.

In actual fact, the family system itself cannot be conceived without its territory. When we think of our own families, we spontaneously imagine the vertical representation of a genealogical tree descending down through time until it reaches us. But our parents, grandparents and great-grandparents must have lived in the same places if they were to meet and marry. *A family system is, in reality, a set of families exchanging spouses within a certain territory.* Even in the so-called 'endogamous' systems of the Arab world or south India, the majority of spouses are not first-degree cousins, and territory, just as much as the family, ensures matrimonial exchange and the perpetuation of values. In certain cases, admittedly, religion can act as a symbolic place and enable exchanges between spouses at a distance, most often between well-off families. But even in the Jewish people, most marriages in bygone days occurred in the same district or the same ghetto.

The concept of a memory of places is liberating. It means we can accept the permanence of regional cultures and national cultures without confining human beings in some immutable essence. Just as Picardy, Brittany and Provence can continue to exist without there being any stock type of Picards, Bretons or Provençaux violently separated by strong values instilled into them in childhood, so too England, Sweden and Germany can all be thoroughly well-established countries without us having to suppose that there is some caricature of an English, Swedish or German person separated from the rest of the world by their upbringing.

A reduction ad absurdum will enable us to understand, conversely, that family values strongly implanted into people's minds would, with high levels of migration, lead to a disintegration of territories and the impossibility of any family system being able to perpetuate itself. If family values were, as the 'psychoanalytical' model would have it, deeply lodged within children's brains, migrations would bring families that are impermeable to assimilation right into the heart of the host societies. The increasing number of immigrants would entail the creation of little islands that continued to diverge from the original culture of the place. These islands may seem to exist for periods at a time, but Little Italy and China Town were just landing strips, decompression chambers in which the first generation to arrive could adapt to its new environment, after the shake-up entailed by the transferral of one culture to another. Immigrants at all times and in all places are destined – if the host society does not prevent them – to become citizens of their new country. Irrespective of the multiculturalist discourse on the respect for difference, the fact of the matter is that all individuals, wherever they may be, and even if they wish to remain as faithful as possible to what they have inherited from their families, aspire above all to become ordinary people just like those around them. This mechanism is particularly powerful among children and teenagers. The educational struggle of certain families against the school or the local district is generally speaking a battle lost in advance. Cultures have to be separated out into territories if they are to endure. In this respect, the current situation in France does not seem to be fundamentally different from that in other countries, but in the case of France we need to bear in mind the difficulties entailed by an absurd or perverse economic management – one that at all events has the effect of segregating people. We need to be fully aware of the way that the responsibility for the failure of assimilation, if failure there is, always lies with the host society, never with immigrant groups: it is unlikely that the latter will refuse to assimilate, but it is always possible that the host population will reject them.

Everything indicates that, in Paris, there are mimetic mechanisms of assimilation at work, but in a fragmented way: we cannot exclude the hypothesis that there is an ongoing transformation of the values of the upper social strata that comprise more than a quarter of the population there.

There is no reason why liberty should, in Paris, suffer any inroads due to the historical and sociological context. Liberty is, if anything, treated with hysterical respect. Contemporary hyperindividualism, the 'culture of narcissism', in

Christopher Lasch's terms,[1] leads to the atomization of society, and an uncertainty as to the final purposes of existence. Is the individual really any freer in this environment, which tends to anomie and the absence of any collective signposts rather than to a flourishing life? It is difficult to tell. One thing is sure: the isolation of individual minds and the emotional needs that flow therefrom contributed greatly to the mass fusion of 11 January 2015. Too much individuality sometimes kills the individual. But this would lead to a potential pathology of liberty rather than an authoritarian transformation of the system of values.

It is the deactivation of the value of equality in the Paris region, in ideology as in political behaviour, that we need to understand. The new stratification of education, which lies behind the emergence of an inegalitarian social subconscious, is fully operational in the Île-de-France. Paris is, par excellence, the city of the higher and lower managerial classes: they comprise 28 per cent of the active population here, as against 24 per cent in Toulouse and 18–20 per cent in most of the great provincial cities. The high degree of educational verticalization in the Île-de-France abolishes the egalitarian anthropological effect. It allows each of the strata – the primary, the secondary, and the higher – to live turned in on itself to become, as it were, a territory, itself prone to fall apart. The well-off person from the liberal professions, the 'bobo' (bourgeois-bohemian), the person who lives in the suburbs or the inner city, all become types set apart, geographically separated from the others – even if everyone still perhaps reproduces, in their environment, liberal and egalitarian values. The fact remains that, these days, the existence of differentiated educational levels is producing an eclipse of the

[1] Christopher Lasch, *The Culture of Narcissism: American Life in an Age of Diminishing Expectations* (London: Abacus, 1980).

egalitarian Parisian temperament. Can we go so far as to say
that the egalitarian unconscious of the anthropological system
is being undermined in the mass of the upper strata? The
truth is that we do not know. The combination of old family
values and a new educational stratification, the separation
into territories that are socio-professional more than ethnic,
the way that the categories of educated Parisians are being
flooded by waves of new graduates of zombie Catholic origin,
the increasing influx of new graduates of immigrant origin –
all these factors are creating a confused situation. Even if our
grasp of the mechanism by which values are reproduced were
enriched by the hypothesis of weak values that make strong
systems possible, we still cannot say whether the value of
equality is at present collapsing in the Parisian middle classes.
The very high level of participation in the 11 January demonstration might suggest the answer 'yes', but the existence
of two competing xenophobias in France, the 'differentialist'
xenophobia rooted in the principle of inequality and the 'universalist xenophobia' rooted in the principle of equality – I
will be comparing them in my next chapter – does not allow
us to say what really motivated the Paris demonstration.

Conversely, the political developments of the last thirty
years have been such as to suggest that the value of equality is intact in the lower-class milieus of *la France centrale*,
where, since the 1980s, it has unfortunately produced a scary
wave of 'universalist xenophobia'. However, this wave is
merely the fall-out of the dominant trend towards inequality
in French society.

The four stages of the crisis

Now that we have analysed the main elements in the drama,
we can sum up, in plain and simple terms, the way ideology

in France has shifted from the principle of equality towards its opposite:

1 To begin with there exist, in the upper classes narrowly defined, and in the bastions of Catholicism, stable cornerstones for the value of inequality.

2 The latest bout of de-Christianization is producing a rise in the power of the zombie Catholic third of the periphery and its inegalitarian substrate.

3 The upper classes, whether zombie Catholics or not, are swollen by the development of education and extending their influence downwards, by capillary action: this influence may involve, if not the value of inequality, at least an ill-defined set of inegalitarian feelings.

4 The European mechanism, whose centre of gravity is slipping northwards and towards the principle of inequality, is becoming a major point of support for the forces of inequality in France. Conversely, the inegalitarian third of the French provinces and an ill-defined part of its middle classes are transmitting a principle of inequality that is being deployed at the European level under German leadership.

At this stage, it is clearly tempting to refer to Vichy (the self-dissolution of the French Republic into a continental Europe under German hegemony), but this would be a gross oversimplification. On the eve of French defeat in 1940, there was no observable rise of the Catholic periphery, and no measurable development in higher education. On the contrary: the Popular Front had demonstrated the vitality of the egalitarian principle in the country, and the weakness of the upper strata of society. A perception of the continuity of territories and human groups should not lead us to the 'false' conception of an immobile history.

4

The French of the Far Right

One of the most powerful of scientific research tools is the principle of symmetry. It is rare for a stable system not to include balances in which forces and forms mirror one another, as elements in an overall structure in which an aberration in one sense, A, will inevitably find its counterpart in an aberration in the opposite sense, minus A. So it would be surprising if the absurdity of a French Republic now firmly rooted in its inegalitarian anthropological structures were not mirrored by the symmetric absurdity of an officially xenophobic force rooted in an egalitarian anthropological background. This force is very easy to identify in the case of France: it is the National Front, which affirms the inferiority of immigrants and their children, but whose geographical basis is increasingly clearly located in the regions that created the French Revolution.

The slow march of the National Front towards *la France centrale*

We live with the National Front. Since 1988, journalists have vied with one another in commenting on the gradual submersion of the French political system by a far right whose overall advance has in fact been moderate. Jean-Marie Le Pen won 14.4 per cent of the votes in the presidential elections of 1988, Marine Le Pen won 17.9 per cent in the same elections in 2012. A 3.5 per cent rise in a quarter of a century is not exactly a meteoric rise. And yet there is no doubt that the grip of the National Front on one part of French society has increased. But its slow progress masks, more than it reveals, a structural transformation. The ideological development of its governing group is not altogether convincing – I personally doubt that, in its heart of hearts, it has really abandoned an anti-Semitism that comes from the differentialist periphery of the French system. But the way the far right is now rooted in the working class represents a new phenomenon in the history of France. It could be observed as early as the late 1980s.

Be this as it may, the real novelty of the last ten years resides in the geographical movement of the National Front vote: it began in the eastern third of the national territory, with a large immigrant population, and it is gradually shifting towards the centre of France. The coefficient of correlation linking the far right vote and the proportion of immigrants of Algerian, Moroccan and/or Tunisian nationality fell from +0.79 in 1986 to +0.10 in 2012. The far right, which has long had support among ordinary people, is seeking and gradually finding its ideal anthropological basis. *Le Mystère français* emphasized the tendency of the National Front to establish itself in the egalitarian central space. A detailed cartographical analysis did, however, reveal this tendency as early as 1993. All that was needed then was to identify, using a statistical regression analysis, the *départements* in which the National Front's score was higher than what might have been expected from the proportion of immigrants of North African origin in the population.

Map 4.1, which charts these deviations, shows us with

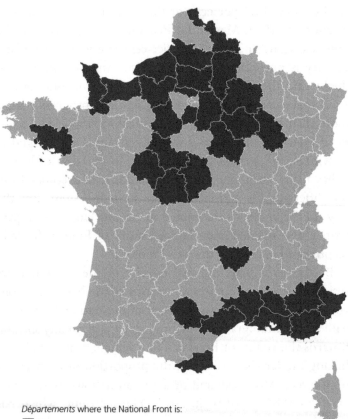

Départements where the National Front is:
■ higher
▨ lower
than what might be expected from the
number of immigrants from North Africa

Map 4.1   The National Front and equality in 1993

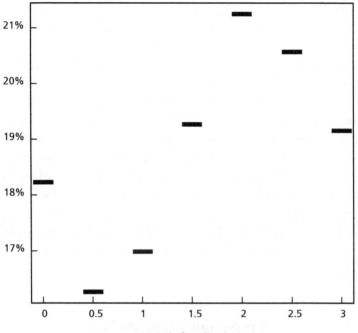

*Figure 4.1   Vote for Le Pen, first round of the presidential
elections 2012*

startling clarity that, already in 1993, the National Front vote
was abnormally high in the egalitarian zone, in the regions
that were at the heart of the French Revolution.[1]

Meanwhile, Figure 4.1 indicates how the vote for Marine
Le Pen (in 2012) varies with the latent egalitarianism of
the anthropological system. The far right obtains its worst
results where the index of equality by *département*, as defined
in Chapter 1 above, is just 0.5; its best results come where
the same index is 2. If we combine total inequality and high
inequality (indices 0 and 0.5), we obtain a National Front

[1] Emmanuel Todd, *Le Destin des immigrés* (Paris: Seuil, 1994), pp. 308–12.

vote of 17.1 per cent, if we combine high, very high and maximum equality (2, 2.5 and 3), we get 20 per cent. In short, irrespective of all local political, social and economic vagaries, the National Front vote is higher in egalitarian territory than in inegalitarian territory.

There is no doubt that National Front electors are moved by feelings that might initially be described as inegalitarian, resting on the desire to push down to the bottom of society, or to its outskirts, individuals and groups perceived as less French, or not French at all. However, an egalitarian unconscious still seems to be at work within them. Once the 'republican' anthropological base of the far right electorate has been identified, it becomes easier to explain how it can reject the authority of governing groups and self-proclaimed elites.

A perversion of universalism

It is not clear that we can interpret the hostility felt towards populations of North African origin on the part of manual workers and small shopkeepers, which form the big battalions of the National Front vote, in terms of racism, i.e. as the effect of a fundamental belief in the existence of essentialized categories of human beings. In France, structurally speaking, there is a high rate of mixed marriages, including in populations of non-European origin. I will trace their recent development in my next chapter. In every period, our nation has been different in this respect from the Protestant and multicultural countries of Northern Europe. Of course, these mixed marriages especially affect lower-class milieus that are more in contact with immigrant groups than are the middle classes. But how can we combine in one satisfying explanation the hostility to populations of Arab origin *and* the acceptance of mixed marriage? The concept of a 'perversion of universalism' will help here.

Let us begin with the psychological sequence defined by an egalitarian family structure: 'Brothers are equal, human beings are equal, peoples are equal.' What happens when there is a confrontation with foreigners? At the moment of contact, there is always a discordance between the principle of the egalitarian system and the reality of a visible difference; the more significant this concrete difference, the more violent the reaction. The difference from the North African family was initially, from the point of view of anthropology, at a maximum: the traditional Arab family is communitarian, patrilineal and endogamous. It privileges men, shuts away women, and prefers marriage between first cousins, at statistical rates approaching, until around 2000, 25 per cent in Morocco, 28 per cent in Algeria and 35 per cent in Tunisia. (Currently, these rates are falling rapidly in North Africa.)

The universalist principle of the system found in *la France centrale* does make it possible to weave fine theories, such as that embodied tacitly in the Universal Declaration of Human Rights, and an equally impressive practice of assimilation of immigrants by marriage. But it can also lead, in the intervening phases, to retrenchments of extreme violence. Let us take the egalitarian principle to its logical conclusion: 'If human beings are the same everywhere, if the foreigners setting foot on our soil behave in ways that really are different, the reason is that they are not really human beings.'

I remember a joke told by a member of the audience after a lecture where I had put forward this explanation, around 1995. 'Yes, in Béziers, we put it differently: racism is just like the Arabs – it shouldn't exist.' The universalism of expulsion or extermination is not, in theory, inconceivable. In practice, the appearance of children who speak French, whether or not they are the products of mixed marriages, swiftly places an obstacle in the way of this theoretical possibility. The fact remains that the National Front vote typically results from a literal interpretation of the dogma of the universal human being. It very quickly expressed the exasperation of a populace that could not imagine anything other than a swift assimilation and was forced to note that it was taking time to absorb certain differences. Furthermore, at the decisive time when the National Front emerged, a certain discourse on tolerance came clattering down from the elites towards the French lower classes: this discourse – completely dysfunctional – stated the necessity of respecting the difference of immigrants. Thus it was that, at the very same time as the lower classes were worried by the slowness of assimilation, their rulers were proclaiming that this assimilation was not necessary. The 'right to difference', a right produced by the upper echelons of society, was just as 'necessary' to the genesis of the National Front as the confrontation, at ground level, between a feminist, exogamous host culture and a patrilineal, endogamous immigrant culture. The combination of lower-class egalitarianism and the multiculturalism of the elites had, at the start of the 1980s, brought together the ideal conditions for a pathological crystallization. The chemical product that emerged from the test tube was the National Front vote.

Throughout this analysis of the movement of the lower-class electorate towards the far right, it has never been a question of Islam, but rather of the actual Arab way of life. In fact, the main growth of the National Front occurred at a time when Islam, an abstract religious or ideological form, was a major preoccupation in hardly anyone's mind. The concept of Islamophobia does not really apply to the period between 1980 and 1990. Arabophobia would be a more accurate term. And this is perfectly logical. 'Universalist xenophobia' focuses on concrete, visible differences in customs and manners. 'Differentialist xenophobia', which thinks that the other is in principle different, can however manage without the reality – but it does need, in order to designate the object of its attentions, an abstract and ideally religious label. Thus it is that, with the development of differentialist concerns in the middle classes, the Muslim has replaced the Arab in dominant representations. Clearly, the coexistence of the two logics in a single ideological space has led to their partial fusion and means that it is very difficult indeed to distinguish between them. However, nothing stops us imagining a possible separation in the future. Arabophobia, lower-class and egalitarian in motivation, and Islamophobia, bourgeois and inegalitarian, are two very different things. Also, it is not self-evident that lower-class milieus, currently in a state of revolt against their middle and upper classes, have any passionate desire to share a phobia with those classes. As a good grasp of social physics will tell us, nothing stops us imagining an Islamophobia of the privileged that would end up making Arabophobia seem aberrant to manual workers and employees.

However, we should not imagine that Arabs have been the sole victims of this perversion of universalism that can lead people to declare that foreigners, as different, are non-human. In 1914, in Paris, the Germans were viewed as a species of animal. Long before them, it was the English who were deprived of their status as *Homo sapiens* by the French revolutionaries. Here is Robespierre, on 11 pluviôse of Year II, speaking at the Club des Jacobins: 'As a Frenchman, a representative of the people, I declare that I hate the English.' Five months later, the decree of 7 prairial, Year II, states: 'No English or Hanoverian prisoner is to be taken.'[1] Defined

---

[1] Sophie Wahnich, *L'Impossible Citoyen. L'étranger dans le discours de la Révolution française* (Paris: Albin Michel, 1997).

as free by its constitution, the English people were responsible for their actions: their opposition to revolutionary France was incomprehensible and meant they were no longer part of the human race. As might perhaps have been expected, the Convention's decree was not applied by the revolutionary armies in the field. Xenophobia of the universalist kind is fragile and unstable by nature, ceaselessly threatened by the possibility that it will have to make a bumpy landing on the real ground of women and men who are, after all, just women and men. A rather good illustration of the ideal type of this intrinsic fragility would be, in contemporary France, the quite common case of the National Front activist who moves in with a pretty girl of North African origin, and tears up his party card.

France did not wait for de-Christianization and the Revolution to produce an aggressive form of universalism. The Catholicism of the Paris Basin – when this Catholicism was still a living force, in the sixteenth or seventeenth century for example – was egalitarian and universalist, in a violent mode. In France, Protestants were – even earlier than the Vendée royalists or the English of 1793 – the object of the reductive fever of the central system. French Protestantism, particularly well established in the peripheral provinces dominated by stem families in the south, was, after a long struggle, practically eradicated by a Catholicism whose main territory was the heart of the Paris Basin and which prefigured the Revolution in its ideal of liberty and metaphysical equality. As for Calvinist predestination, it had seduced the stem families of Occitania, which were accustomed to designating first-born sons as their heirs and did not believe in either liberty or equality.

The Revolution spread the universalist and reductive mind-set of *la France centrale*, though this ideal finally faded away under the Third Republic, which – faithful to the principles of liberty and equality – eventually ended up tolerating the diversity of the world and, first and foremost, the diversity of France itself. The Catholic community was accepted in the French provinces.

The fact remains that being a universalist does not mean being 'nice'. It means that you operate on the principle that there is a universal human being – us, me! – who is like us, at all times and in all places. If the reality of the world compares this mental system with a human being who is in actual fact different, the universal human being, unwittingly reduced to the purest ethnic status, may react by negating the humanity of the bearer of the contradiction.

Republican anti-Semitism

We can identify a clear attack of universalist xenophobia under the Third Republic, but far from the Paris Basin. In colonial Algeria, there was briefly what might be called a liberal, egalitarian, republican anti-Semitism that I analysed in detail in *Le Destin des immigrés*.[1] Right in the middle of the Dreyfus Affair, Algeria sent to the French Parliament, in May 1898, four 'anti-Jewish' members. The anti-Semitism of the Europeans of North Africa, whether they were of French, Italian or Spanish origin, was not, however, of the same nature as the Catholic anti-Semitism of France itself. In Algeria, the European anthropological backdrop was without any possible doubt liberal, egalitarian and completely secular. The Church had little real influence on the republican colonists. The Algerian Jews were criticized not for assimilating too thoroughly (as the Jews in France were accused of doing), but quite the opposite: they were a bit

[1] Todd, *Le Destin des immigrés*, pp. 331–34.

slow to assimilate and they still practised the communitarian vote. The leaders of the Jewish districts, which remained separated and endogamous communities, negotiated en bloc the votes which they controlled, and hampered a locally individualistic political process. On the national scale, the two anti-Semitisms, the differentialist Catholic version and the universalist republican version, were mixed together.

France's anthropological diversity is most definitely a great advantage – perhaps its ace card. But synthesizing different elements does not always produce good and useful compounds in sociology, any more than it does in chemistry. In Germany between the two world wars, the Protestant regions of the north of the country provided Nazism with its electoral masses, and the regions of the Catholic south gave it its leaders – starting with Hitler. Who would dare to say, these days, that the fusion between the serious inwardness of the Protestants and the imaginative extroversion of the Catholics proved to be a blessing for Germany?

But there are other factors that determine who votes for the National Front beyond egalitarianism, whether this be healthily turned against the higher social categories or, perversely, against foreigners or French people of foreign origin. The new educational stratification plays, as we have seen, an active role in fostering inegalitarianism. In bygone days, communist manual workers, immersed in a society where literacy was universal, gazed up towards the top of the social structure. These workers had in their sights a small upper class whose culture they accepted but whose economic privileges they disputed. They were marching towards the future. The people who vote National Front see above them the crushing mass of a middle class defined by its educational attainments. They no longer dream of achieving the same status. They look downwards, filled with the fear of being dragged down. Their anger is turned against immigrants.

Educational development has shaken the ideal of equality, particularly in *la France centrale*, and especially in its lower-class milieus. But we need to keep in mind the existence of an increasingly strong link between the National Front and the egalitarian anthropological backdrop. Translated into the common language of politics, this comes down to saying that when the leaders of the National Front say their party is republican, they are not talking complete nonsense. Robespierre's anti-English remarks have just reminded us that republican universalism is not always friendly to foreigners as real human beings.

So everyone claims to be republican these days, in a France drifting ever further from the value of equality, and we are going to need to work with a more precise terminology. I gave the label 'neo-republican' to that part of the system of political representation ('the so-called republican parties') that accepts a logic of exclusion rooted in implicitly inegalitarian values. I will give the label 'post-republican' to the National Front, which may have been produced by egalitarian anthropological structures but seems to have moved beyond them with its ethnically fixated and xenophobic ideology.

But the anthropological analysis has other surprises in store for us. It does not confirm the National Front's vision of a homogeneous UMPS.[1] The Socialist Party and the Union for a Popular Movement have different relations to equality – and these relations are quite different from what might have been expected.

---

[1] The UMP (Union pour un mouvement populaire) – the centre-right party in France – is often amalgamated, in National Front propaganda, with the PS or Parti socialiste, to produce the acronym UMPS, the implication being that there is no real difference between the mainstream right-wing and left-wing parties. (Translator's note.)

Le Pen, Sarkozy and equality

The spatial distribution of the Le Pen vote in the first round of the presidential election in 2012 (Map 4.2) shows that the National Front's movement towards the egalitarian space of *la France centrale* is continuing. For the time being, its maximum zones of strength, northeast of the Paris Basin, with an

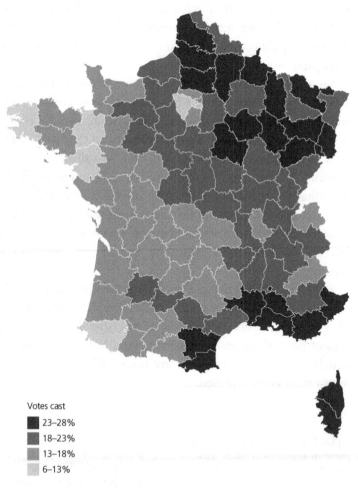

Votes cast

- ■ 23–28%
- ■ 18–23%
- ■ 13–18%
- ■ 6–13%

Map 4.2   Le Pen 2012

epicentre in the Champagne region, not to mention Provence, are similar to the main area of the French Revolution. Election after election, there is an increasing tension within the National Front between an ideology that affirms a principle of inequality and the inferiority of immigrants, and an egalitarian factor determining who votes for the party.

To anyone familiar with the map of the inegalitarian Catholic bastions on the periphery, the distribution of the Sarkozy vote in the first round of the 2012 presidential election is even more surprising (Map 4.3). What we see here is a large number of residues of the Catholic right in Savoy, Alsace, the Vendée, Mayenne and even throughout the inland areas of the west of France. But Sarkozy also won a very large share of the vote in Provence and in the heart of the Paris Basin, in the revolutionary heartlands. In short, as Figure 4.2 shows, he won the greatest number of votes

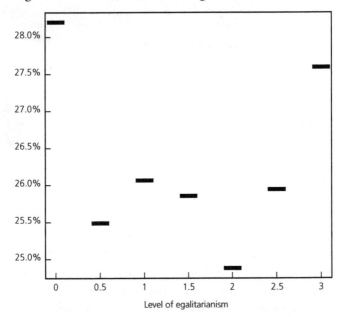

Figure 4.2   The Sarkozy vote, 1st round 2012

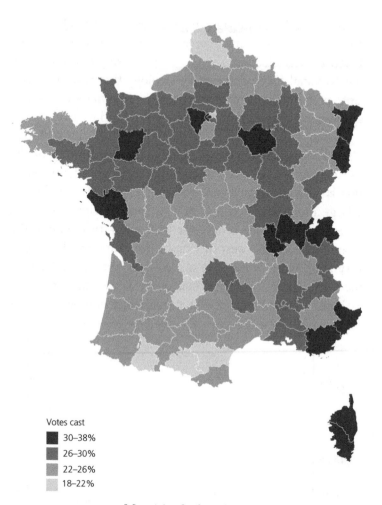

Votes cast
■ 30–38%
■ 26–30%
■ 22–26%
■ 18–22%

Map 4.3   Sarkozy 2012

simultaneously in the zones with both the lowest *and* the highest levels of egalitarianism. The anthropological variable common to his political space overall seems to be the degree with which the nuclear family predominates – this is a factor both in the inland west of France, which was until very recently Catholic, and the heart of the Paris Basin, as well as Provence, which both used to be republican. This overall geographical base would define the electorate for the neo-republican right as being fundamentally individualist. However, the main point here is the emergence of a UMP that has put down strong roots in the egalitarian zone. We should note that, in the second round of the 2012 presidential elections, the lower-class milieus of the Picardy and Champagne-Ardenne regions gave Sarkozy a majority against François Hollande, the candidate of the 'left'.[1] The French political system of representation does look really rather odd, with these far-right (post-republican) and right-wing (neo-republican) electorates both being, under the surface, egalitarian. Hence the rather comic side of the situation: what brings the National Front closest to the UMP, over and above their respective leaders being on the right, is a shared egalitarian anthropological base. This explains why the right finds it so difficult to carry out 'reforms' when it is in power. Its individualist, nuclear family-oriented base encourages it to carry out such reforms, but its unconscious egalitarian roots resist all attempts to attain the nirvana of neoliberal politics, the undermining of the welfare state.

The Socialist Party and inequality: the concept of objective xenophobia

The supporters of inequality can rest assured that the Socialist Party is there to embody, one day, perhaps, their craziest ideological dreams.

Let us stay faithful to the scientific tool of symmetry, here applied to the ideological space of France. The existence of an egalitarian right means we are obliged to seek

---

[1] Hervé Le Bras and Emmanuel Todd, *Le Mystère français*, p. 270.

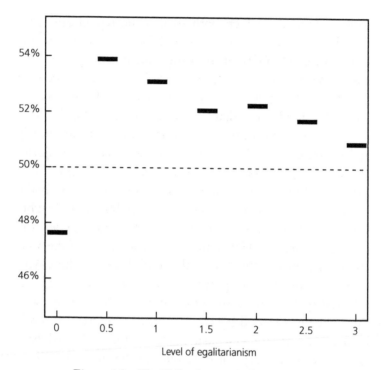

Figure 4.3   The Hollande vote, 2nd round 2012

for an inegalitarian Socialist Party – and we shall find it. Figure 4.3 shows the degree to which the anthropological base of the French left is now far removed from its revolutionary origins. As seen in Figures 4.1 and 4.2, but this time in the context of the second round of the presidential elections, the average share of the vote for Hollande is calculated separately for *départements* with different levels of anthropological egalitarianism.

On level of equality 0, what we find is a very low vote, the last point of resistance to socialist inroads – an effect of the specific implantation of the right in Alsace. But at 0.5, the vote for François Hollande reaches its highest level, then decreases at a regular rate as the level of egalitarianism rises

(Figure 4.3). Indeed, it is also worth underlining the fact that it is the level of the Sarkozy vote that rises with the level of egalitarianism.

The cartography of the Hollande vote confirms these results (Map 4.4). The partly de-Christianized regions of stem families in the southwest of France and the zones

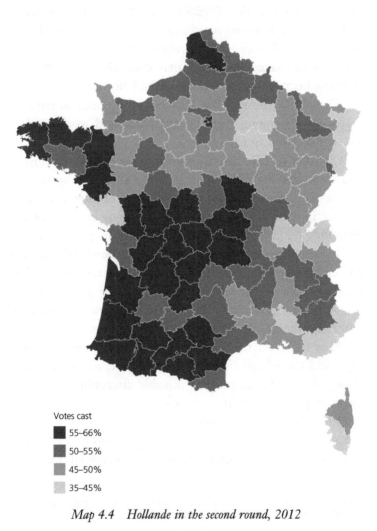

Votes cast

■ 55–66%
■ 50–55%
■ 45–50%
□ 35–45%

Map 4.4   Hollande in the second round, 2012

where the nuclear family is less strong, and where egalitarianism is at a low level, in the north, can again be clearly seen on the map and were already among the traditional bastions of the SFIO.[1] But the neo-republican Socialist Party has lost the egalitarian Bouches-du-Rhône and has extended southwards into the bastions of the Catholic right in the Hautes-Pyrénées, the Pyrénées-Atlantiques, the Aveyron and the Lot. It has conquered most of Brittany. Only Maine-et-Loire, the Vendée, and Mayenne resist it. Of course, this could be explained by saying that these three *départements* were the heart of the movement of the Chouans who resisted the French Revolution. But what we really need to stress is that they are among the most industrial and working-class areas in the west of France.

It is time to take this argument to its logical conclusion and to accept the ultimate consequences of the hypothesis of a Socialist Party aligned with the value of inequality. The implications of this anthropological analysis in terms of the economy are evident: the Socialist Party in power continues to be on the side of the wealthy and the elderly, after it had campaigned on behalf of the poor and the young. The consequences of our discovery, if we are to grasp Socialist discourse and practice in the area of immigration, are even more significant. As we approach the shores of truth, we need, as social scientists, to be as faithful as possible to the logic and the ethical rigour of Max Weber, and seek to disclose, albeit with the greatest possible discretion, the values latent in political action.

Officially, since the 1980s, the Socialist Party has been the defender of immigrants and their children. Its 'antiracism' stance is a constant factor. It sponsored the SOS

---

[1] Section Française de l'Internationale Ouvrière – the former name of the Socialist Party in France. (Translator's note.)

Racisme movement with its slogan 'Touche pas à mon pote' ('Hands off my pal') and from time to time it still suggests that foreigners should have the right to vote in local elections. However, this commitment was, right from the start, part of a multiculturalist logic that insists on the 'right to difference', which is a clinical symptom, so to speak, of a deep-rooted inegalitarian unconscious. This cannot really surprise us: in the 1970s and 1980s, the Socialist Party was energized by new cadres and electorates from the Catholic periphery. The 'right to difference' is the normal form of the way post-Catholic milieus manage immigrants. For its proponents it works quite well in periods of prosperity, especially if foreigners have not yet become too French. But in difficult times, when the unemployment rate goes up and there is a strong drive towards assimilation, the initially benevolent differentialist mentality turns sinister, and in the new unclear situation finds it easy to point to the existence of a kind of apartheid, as Manuel Valls did in January 2015. The rates of mixed marriages in France show that such a word is nonsensical here: the definition of apartheid in South Africa made one of its main stipulations a ban on interracial marriages. But it makes no difference: the concept exists, carefully stored away on the differentialist mental shelves, ready to be taken down and used – for apartheid is the true horizon of multiculturalism.

Manuel Valls was born in Barcelona, one of the centres of Iberian differentialism. In this city and its hinterlands, nationalism is currently on the rise, and threatens to break up Spain. The peasants of Catalonia traditionally lived in very pure types of stem families: the *hereu* or designated heir is still a cultural stereotype. So the sequence 'inequality of brothers, inequality of peoples' is particularly evident in Catalonia – to such an extent that it comprises a small nation, impelled by a mentality of defence rather than of conquest.

A person can never be defined simply by anthropological criteria. All we can verify are the statistical implications that lead, for instance, from the predominance within a human group of the family principle of inequality to the preference, in that same group, of a politics of difference. The fact remains that imagining Catalonia to be part of the genealogy of the use of the word 'apartheid' in France is frankly comical.

Be this as it may, we need to be wary of Socialist benevolence towards immigrants and their children. This benevolence does without any doubt include a residual authentic universalism – the universalism which expects and demands the pure and simple assimilation of the foreigner, as an individual, into the central culture. But these days, the French left is also imbued with an unconscious differentialist substrate that has no particular desire to see the children of Arabs, Blacks and Jews becoming citizens like everyone else. This substrate feels intellectually justified when it sees that there are *beurs*[1] who are terrorists, Blacks who go in for rap, and Jews who wear the kippa.

Let us leave high-minded speeches to one side and move on to objective facts. From this point of view, it appears that the Socialists' economic management (which has stayed the same since they took power in 1983: the strong franc, then the march to the euro and the defence of the euro) traps whole districts in unemployment – the same districts that are, according to Manuel Valls, threatened by apartheid. *This management is the main brake on the assimilation of immigrants' children because it stops a great many of them projecting themselves, in practical and psychological terms, into a decent future.* At this stage in our argument, we need to maintain the (quite likely) hypothesis that the socialist leaders, cadres

[1] French people of North African descent. (Translator's note.)

and activists are all endowed with a normal intelligence. And it is patently obvious, for any normal intelligence, that an economic policy that is a carbon copy of that of Germany (a country that, in proportion, produces 35 per cent fewer children than France) condemns a high number of young French people to unemployment. It is also perfectly evident that those young people who are least in tune with the national system of privileges, those who are the children of the latest arrivals in the country, suffer the harmful effects of this policy more than do the others. *In other words, while the Socialist Party talks about integration, it has chosen, with its economic policy, to enforce segregation.* The simplicity of this logical sequence and the obstinacy shown in putting it into practice are such that this simply cannot be just an accident or a piece of bad luck.

Of course, we cannot say that the Socialist Party *wants* to trap the children of immigrants in exclusion. But we need at least to admit that this entrapment is accepted, and that the dominant party on the French left does not view itself as being responsible for the well-being and the future of this part of the population. So what we are dealing with here is a profound differentialism, which follows routes that may be indirect, though I could not in all honesty claim that they are completely unconscious. To commit a wrong, all you need to do, most of the time, is to look away.

At this point, we need a terminology that will allow us to distinguish between the xenophobic vociferations of the National Front, which have no impact on the economic life of the suburbs, and Socialist economic practice, which *really* contributes to the exclusion of the great masses of immigrants' children from the French nation.

The xenophobia of National Front voters is conscious, deliberate, self-assertive: it is a 'subjective xenophobia'. The xenophobia of the Socialist Party, laid bare by its economic behaviour even if it is denied by the official policies, can be designated as an 'objective xenophobia'.

Let us sum up:

- The Socialist Party is *objectively xenophobic*. Rooted in inegalitarian anthropological structures, it is differentialist and does not really wish to see all the children of immigrants entering the nation.
- The National Front electorate is *subjectively xenophobic*. It is the product of egalitarian anthropological structures and cannot in practical terms tolerate the existence of immigrants as a different category.

From the point of view of scientific logic and the principle of symmetry, the world is now sorted. As for the lives of French people, that is a different matter. The objective xenophobia of economic policy keeps immigrants, and especially their children, in a visibly different category. Thus it untiringly fosters the subjective xenophobia of National Front electors, who are exasperated by the 'difference' of foreigners and by their 'refusal to assimilate'.

Here we find ourselves facing – as in the case of the outbreak of anti-Semitism at the end of the nineteenth century, but in another way – one of those complex ideological combinations that are made possible by the anthropological diversity of France. The differentialist motivations of the periphery and the universalist motivations of the centre collaborate in the emergence of an admittedly mixed but still very menacing form of racism. The image that comes to mind is that of a particularly dangerous virus resulting from the recombination of two distinct strands of DNA.

A study of the National Front in the anthropological space of France would be incomplete without an investigation of the party that would like to supplant it but cannot do so, namely the Left Front (Front de gauche).[1] The same method of analysis, applied this time to the vote for Jean-Luc Mélenchon in 2012, will shed further light on the situation.

Mélenchon and inequality

Jean-Luc Mélenchon obtained 11.1 per cent of the vote in the first round of the 2012 presidential elections. Unlike with the electors of François Hollande, a true 'lower-class' bias was clear in the exit polls carried out on this occasion. Both manual workers and jobless were strongly represented in the electorate – which is only logical, given the Communist Party's support for the Left Front candidate. But any explanation for the Mélenchon phenomenon, in the politically favourable context of an oppression of the working classes, must lie in grasping how he failed to attract the popular vote in the same way that the National Front has.

On the political level, the absence of any really radical economic approach, and the refusal to advocate a plain and simple exit from the Eurozone, were probably enough to identify Mélenchon as yet one more variety of socialist candidate, with the usual mixture of grand principles and the absence of any concrete proposals. While his electorate here clearly bears the mark of the working-class communist world, the cadres and active fellow-travellers of Mélenchon are close to the world of the civil service or more precisely to the French-style social state, run by and for the middle classes.

---

[1] A federation of left-wing parties to the left of the Socialist Party; its president is Jean-Luc Mélenchon. It includes anti-capitalist and ecological strands, and tends to Euroscepticism. (Translator's note.)

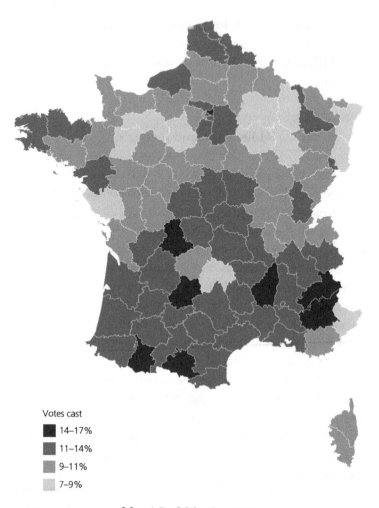

Map 4.5   Mélenchon 2012

The map of the Mélenchon vote speaks for itself (Map 4.5). We can clearly see the trace of the influence of the French Communist Party, in the Nord-Pas-de-Calais, the Paris region, the northwest edges of the Massif Central and the Côtes d'Armor. But what is most striking is the way it is generally established in the areas occupied by the Occitanian

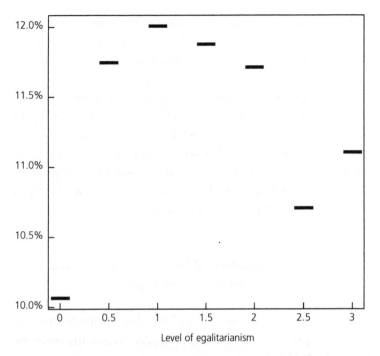

Figure 4.4   The Mélenchon vote, 1st round 2012

stem family – a fraternal mixture of *départements* that were, traditionally, more or less secularized and zombie Catholic *départements*, such as the Pyrénées-Atlantiques, the Aveyron, the Lozère, the Haute-Loire and Savoy. This is the world of stem families and inequality, an authoritarian inequality that likes vertical structures, the State and the Church for example. Only Alsace, somewhat deaf to the demand for the abolition of the Concordat,[1] is missing from this list.

The same phenomenon can be described in negative terms. Populism of the Mélenchon kind has failed to seduce the great Paris Basin, that egalitarian, individualist area. Figure 4.4 reveals that the vote has dropped where egalitarian

---

[1] See above, p. 62. (Translator's note.)

values are at their strongest. From the anthropological point of view, Jean-Luc Mélenchon has not managed to find the central revolutionary space, as Marine Le Pen has, and his republican fundamentalism is running idle.

We are back to square one. We showed, above, that the right and the far right were linked, under the surface, by an egalitarian anthropological backdrop, and now we are finding that the left and the far left are joined together by the value of inequality. For lack of any consolation of a religious or ideological kind, we can draw, from this crazy symmetry, a sense of well-being of an aesthetic kind.

The insignificance of human beings and the violence of ideologies

I am perfectly aware that the anthropological model that has just been presented is not easy to accept. While the maps are very clear, the differences in political scores between areas with varying levels of egalitarianism are not so huge.

An interpretation of these nuances can draw on symbolic rejection and economic destruction. It seems to suggest not just a very great violence and a vast amount of bad faith on the part of those involved, but also a degree of conviction, determination and force. We can just about imagine such sentiments animating those elected on the far right, or Muslim fundamentalists or militant atheists. But are they conceivable among people who think of themselves as centre left?

President François Hollande, for example, is a good-natured fellow, insignificant, 'normal', to use his own term. The Socialists are moderate in all things. Our theory therefore seems not really to be compatible with the obvious fact that these are people with little inclination towards brutality, with lukewarm beliefs and a rather flabby political commitment. So we still need to understand how low-intensity inegalitarian and differentialist preferences can lead, collectively, to an obstinacy of unusual violence.

Our meditations in the previous chapter on the way weak family values can produce strong systems will guide us towards an explanation. What we find amongst all the neo-republicans – Socialists, UMP members, centrists and members of the Left Front – is a set of weak beliefs whose strength lies in the fact that they are common to entire milieus in the same way that family values are common to certain territories.

Groups that subscribe to particular values are not all defined by the context of a *département* or a town or city. But a particular physical way of being part of space – a village, a town, a district, a professional network, a political party – is necessary for there to be daily interactions between individuals, giving life to their beliefs and their behaviour. A milieu is maintained largely by mimetic phenomena that have nothing to do with intense beliefs. The values that it brings to life, and that define it, may concern important or insignificant elements in personal and social life.

I now realize that my first contact with the collective power of weak values predated my analysis of the perpetuation of family systems in the urban environment. Basically, I started out from ideology. Between 1992 and 1995, I noticed that it was not impossible to demonstrate to a pro-European, in a face-to-face discussion, that the single currency was an absurd project, but belief in the inevitability of the euro was, on a collective level, invulnerable. The weak belief was already fostered by a social group sufficiently huge for the individual, after a brief turnabout, to return to his belief, as well as his milieu, after the conversation.

I feel that Daniel Schneidermann had a rather similar intuition when he noted recently, in an article in *Libération*, how obviously insignificant two central figures in the current debates were: Jean-Pierre Jouyet, the star Presidential Chief of Staff, and TV presenter and media star Catherine Barma:

> So here we have two political phenomena: the way public debate has been Zemmourized, and the ideological fusion of what used to be called left and right. And two of the figures who organize and, in the shadows, give shape to these two phenomena, the serial goofball and the woman who has prepared her lesson well, appear under the studio lights without being fully aware of their actions.[1]

François Ruffin has grasped the same thing – or the same nothing – in a fine piece on a Socialist Member of Parliament from Picardy. In *Fakir*, he tells of his 'encounter with the void'.[2]

> For two hours, in her surgery, I talked with my Socialist MP, Pascale Boistard. Rarely have I been given such an empty interview. So I have forgotten it. And yet, I reflected, in all its emptiness, thanks to its emptiness indeed, my interview is evidence of an illness, a collective, degenerative illness.

> Now that the euro has failed, we have a chance to ponder the limit, in the mathematical sense of the term, of the collective aggregation of weak beliefs: on the level of individuals, belief in the single currency tends to zero, while on

---

[1] Daniel Schneidermann, 'Jouyet, Barma, figures de l'ombre en pleine lumière', *Libération*, 16 November 2014.
[2] François Ruffin, *Fakir*, 20 February 2015.

the collective level of the 'elites', it is as strong as ever. We can doubtless put forward the hypothesis of a collective belief that can perpetuate itself even when it exists as an individual belief only as a trace, or not at all. The euro is simply a particular case of systemic inertia, of the persistence of a human project in the absence of any questioning of its validity, quite simply because a certain group exists that originally held a particular belief, and when people as individuals abandon this belief, the belief itself does not die out.

Weak individuals produce strong systems. Someone like François Hollande may hold on to a trace of belief in the single currency, there may be a few dusty residues of a differentialist family tradition, a vague idea that bringing the children of immigrants into the nation is not a priority, is not all that important. But what if you have five hundred thousand François Hollandes rubbing shoulders and copying each other, day after day, or a million or even several million of them? The machinery is all in place: it can fuse belief in the euro and the 'difference of Muslims' together into a formidably obstinate ideology, able to exclude people and destroy lives on a huge scale.

5

The French Muslims

Shortly before he committed suicide in 1941, Stefan Zweig referred in his memoirs to the consternation the Jews felt when they were all grouped together by the Nazis into a category that was by now meaningless for them:

> But the Jews of the twentieth century had for long not been a community. They had no common faith, they were conscious of their Judaism rather as a burden than as something to be proud of and were not aware of any mission. They lived apart from the commandments of their once holy books and they were done with the common language of old. To integrate themselves and become articulated with the people with whom they lived, to dissolve themselves in the common life, was the purpose for which they strove impatiently for the sake of peace from persecution, rest on the eternal flight. Thus the one group no longer understood the other, melted down into other peoples as they were, more Frenchmen, Germans, Englishmen, Russians than they were Jews.

Only now, since they were swept up like dirt in the streets and heaped together, the bankers from their Berlin palaces and sextons from the synagogues of orthodox congregations, the philosophy professors from Paris, and Rumanian cabbies, the undertaker's helpers and Nobel prizewinners, the concert singers, and hired mourners, the authors and distillers, the haves and the have-nots, the great and the small, the devout and the liberals, the usurers and the sages, the Zionists and the assimilated, the Ashkenasim and the Sephardim, the just and the unjust besides which the confused horde who thought that they had long since eluded the curse, the baptized and the semi-Jews – only now, for the first time in hundreds of years, the Jews were forced into a community of interest to which they had long since ceased to be sensitive, the ever-recurring – since Egypt – community of expulsion.[1]

Like the European Jews of around 1930, the Muslims of France do not exist. The religious category is imposed as a common denominator on a group of women and men belonging to different groups, with different national origins, educational levels, jobs and social classes, as well as different degrees and types of religious practice. To stick the label 'Muslim' onto this human diversity is quite simply a racist act, just as sticking the common label 'Jew' onto the bourgeois intellectual of Vienna and the Jew from the shtetl in Poland was a racist act. The soldiers Imad Ibn Ziaten and Mohamed Legouad who were shot down by Mohammed Merah in Montauban were no less 'Muslim' than he was, or than Ahmed Merabet, the policeman who was finished off on the ground by the Kouachi brothers. The problem is of a

---

[1] Stefan Zweig, *Memoirs of Yesterday: Memoirs of a European*, trans. Anthea Bell (London: Pushkin Press, 2014), pp. 427–28.

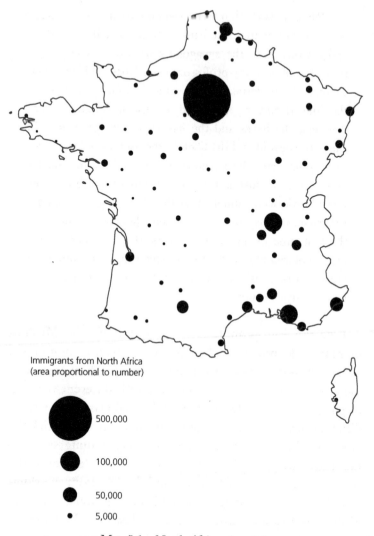

Immigrants from North Africa
(area proportional to number)

500,000

100,000

50,000

5,000

Map 5.1   North African in origin

general nature: the category 'Muslim', in the form in which it is increasingly being used, is a dangerous semantic fiction.

Let us take a look at jobs and socioeconomic categories and see what place the 'Muslims' occupy in the French

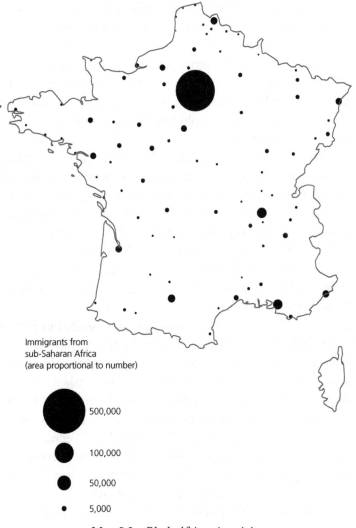

Immigrants from
sub-Saharan Africa
(area proportional to number)

500,000

100,000

50,000

5,000

Map 5.2   Black African in origin

social system: 8.4 per cent of manual workers, 6.4 per cent
of employees, 6.6 per cent of shopkeepers and artisans or
company bosses, 4.5 per cent of lower-middle-class professions, and 3.5 per cent of managerial and liberal professions,

according to an IFOP survey.[1] There is complete social diversity here – nothing to do with the fantasy figure of the young inner-city drop-out, dealing in drugs and always prone to relapse into Islamic terrorism. From this point of view, Christophe Guilluy is right to underline the emergence of a Muslim petty bourgeoisie that is doing quite well, even if he is wrong in apparently deploring this as an injustice against the French lower classes.[2]

Nationalities and educational levels, taken together, confirm the image of a heterogeneous world. Let us first consider the descendants of Algerian immigrants between the ages of 30 and 49 in 2008: 27 per cent have 'no qualifications', 39 per cent have a technical diploma (the 'CAP, BEP or BEPC'), 9 per cent have a 'short' higher education diploma (two years) and 9 per cent a 'long' higher education diploma (BA and above). This last figure – 9 per cent with a 'long' higher level of education – is much lower than the 19 per cent of French people whose ancestors settled in France at an early date, even if it is only slightly higher than the 8 per cent registered for Portuguese descendants. However, this 9 per cent teaches us nothing about 'Islam': among the descendants of parents from Tunisia, the level of those with higher education qualifications rises to 15 per cent. In the case of Moroccan origin, it reaches 19 per cent, i.e. the average of 'true' French people. It is an understatement to say that, sociologically speaking, Islam does not exist, since in this sense North Africa does not exist either.[3]

To be fair, neo-republican France manages to produce, from this impressive educational diversity, a relative equality – at least in unemployment rates: 20 per cent for male

---

[1] Thanks to Jérôme Fourquet for kindly providing me with these figures.
[2] Christophe Guilluy, *La France périphérique. Comment on a sacrifié les milieux populaires* (Paris: Flammarion, 2014).
[3] *Immigrés et descendants d'immigrés en France*, INSEE, 2012, p. 167.

descendants of Algerian immigrants aged between 18 and 50; 22 per cent for those from Tunisia; 21 per cent from sub-Saharan Africa; 22 per cent from Turkey. In view of this absence of correlation between educational level and access to employment, an ill-intentioned social scientist could claim that France is obsessed by religious origin and that qualifications are of no importance here. The new Republic, on this view, is instinctively Islamophobic.[1] We will see that things are a little more complicated.

Local authorities have done their utmost to block the building of mosques. Thus, investigations into Muslim religious practice are seriously incomplete: in the absence of an established network of places of worship, they cannot be based on direct observation. As a result, we do not have, for Islam, sociological surveys of religion of the kind that have made it possible to distinguish between the two great zones that comprise French territory: secular and Catholic. The survey *Trajectoires et origines*, carried out between September 2008 and February 2009, tells us that if 76 per cent of people who define themselves as Catholic consider religion to have little or no importance for them, this level of indifference falls to 52 per cent for Protestants, 53 per cent for Orthodox Christians, 48 per cent for Buddhists, 24 per cent for Jews and 22 per cent for Muslims, with quite similar proportions (as for unemployment rates) for Algerians, Tunisians, Moroccans, Turks and Black Africans.[2] The level given for the Jews, a category familiar to me, tells me that the totally secularized Jews who constitute the majority of the French Jewish population quite simply do not show up in the methodology of the survey, which does not allow for anyone being able to feel Jewish in the absence of any religious belief.

[1] *Trajectoires et origines*, INED and INSEE, Paris, 2011, p. 56.
[2] *Trajectoires et origines*, INED and INSEE, Paris, 2011, p. 127.

So this kind of measurement does not really show us what proportion of the Muslim population is really practising. We know that Ramadan is frequently respected, and that the ban on eating pork is widely observed. Admittedly, we know that the relation to alcohol is much more flexible. Never mind: let us accept that, in current conditions, Muslims in France feel Muslim, and we should congratulate ourselves that the degree of demonization of Islam has not reached such a level that they feel forced to hide their religious attachment. A regular, standardized, complete observance is fairly rare, so we need to ask ourselves whether the self-definition of 78 per cent of respondents as 'Muslims who take their religion seriously' is not quite simply the effect of what I would call the 'Zweig effect': if society as a whole sticks the label 'Muslim' on you, you feel Muslim.

Let us resume the parallel with Jewish history. Around 1930, the majority of Jews of Western Europe were well on their way to forgetting their religious identity. After 1945, any person with one, two, three or four Jewish grandparents knew that being Jewish was not always a matter of personal choice. In short, homogeneity in attachment to the Muslim religion really needs to be related to the homogeneity of unemployment rates, which does not mean, of course, that the experience of unemployment is as dramatic as being sent to a concentration camp.

The disintegration of North African cultures

I hope to have shown, in *Le Destin des immigrés*, that it was absurd to claim you could describe people of Muslim origin within the context of a specific community. The high level in the rates of mixed marriage with the surrounding French society was then proof enough of this fact. The communitarian hypothesis presupposes the perpetuation of a culture with, at its heart, the continuance of a family organization. But what is characteristic of the family from North Africa, or Mali, is precisely the way it disintegrates much more often than it survives. It disintegrates because contacts between the children of immigrants and the children of the host society have been open for a sufficiently long time for fundamental French values, such as the idea of the equality of the sexes – in spite of everything that the media system says – to have been transmitted to the children of Algerians, Tunisians and Moroccans. The illiteracy of the first immigrant generations actually gave the culture of origin no chance.

The father's authority was already traditionally weak in the endogamous communitarian family of origin, since it did not authorize him to choose a husband for his daughter – she was customarily reserved for her patrilineal cousin. But the authority of the illiterate father was quite simply wrecked by the education of a son who had gone to primary school, secondary school or university. Exit 'Muslim culture'. Conversely, the rapidity and violence of the process entailed a significant degree of psychological disorientation and, it has to be said, a fair amount of delinquency. Yes, there are a great number of immigrants' children in prison, but this is precisely because their culture of origin has been fragmented and has failed to protect them, because – irrespective of the labels that society sticks on them or that they stick on themselves – they are not really 'Arabs' or 'Muslims'.

I myself am a typically assimilationist Frenchman, and feel that the fusion of all immigrants into the central culture of the country is a destiny to be wished for. I now have to admit, however, that it has all been going too quickly, that the setting up of a decompression chamber in temporary immigrant cultures – Little Algeria, Morocco Town would have pre-empted a great deal of psychological damage. But you cannot decide on a policy of customs and manners in the way you decide on an economic policy. Given the French preference for assimilation, and the low level of interest shown by this country's women and men for differences in physical appearance, the brutal destruction of North African culture was inevitable.

The fact remains that neither the endogamous communitarian family nor Islam has managed to play, for the second generation born in France, the role of a 'protective covering' in Polanyi's sense. The confrontation with the individualist values of industrial and post-industrial society has been immediate, brutal and destructive. The best comparison, if we are to grasp the disorientation of young people in French suburbs, is not what is happening in the valley of the Euphrates and the desert of Syria, that mirage, that well of violence from another world and another age. Instead, it is what happened in England during the first Industrial Revolution: the brutal deculturation of the manual workers that led to vulnerable families, educational difficulties and alcoholism. For the best qualified of these workers, one route to survival was the Protestantism of the religious sects. When faced with the threat of being destroyed by the market, human beings can find ultimate support in a religious faith that gives them laws to follow and something to hope for.

It is true that the rates of mixed marriage tended to stagnate between the 1992 *Mobilité géographique et insertion sociale* survey (*Geographical mobility and social integration*) and the 2008–9 *Trajectoires et origines* survey (*Trajectories and origins*). Also, the dispersion of populations of North African origin across French territory seems to have come to a halt. These phenomena were both discussed in detail in *Le Mystère français.*[1] It has been the great triumph of Islamophobic commentators, on this point, to pass off the effect as the cause, proclaiming that it is an irreducible cultural difference that is stopping people in the suburbs from adapting: it also explains their unemployment rates. And yet the pause in the rate of assimilation actually results, as we said above, from the decision taken by our ruling classes to tolerate economic stagnation and social fragmentation, a decision accepted and supported by our hegemonic social bloc, the MEZ. As a demographer, I will say it again: as France produces many more children than does Germany, monetary mimicry condemns many of them to difficult, excluded, incomplete lives. Whatever those concerned themselves may think, the executioners as well as their victims, this retreat was not a matter of choice: it has been imposed by an economic logic that blocks the mechanism of assimilation. *The rates of mixed marriage in 1992 showed that things were heading in the right direction. Contrary to what opinion tells us, we observed at that time an unbelievable historical acceleration in the process whereby, in the second half of the twentieth century, populations were mixed together.*

Mixed marriages: Jews and Muslims

Let us compare this with the speed at which Jews are assimilated. As was my mother's habit, I will take a random example – me, or rather, my family. We start with a Jewish family from the east of the country, Alsace or Lorraine; this family was emancipated by the Revolution in 1791. The grandfather of my great-grandmother, Simon Levy, was a chief rabbi in Bordeaux. In 1887, he published *Moïse, Jésus et Mahomet*,

[1] Hervé Le Bras and Emmanuel Todd, *Le Mystère français*, pp. 222–26.

ou les trois grandes religions sémitiques (Moses, Jesus and Muhammad, or the three great Semitic religions),[1] a defence and illustration of the Jewish religion. It was, as ever, about struggling against the calumnies directed against Judaism. Simon Levy points out that the fundamental values of Christianity and Islam descend exclusively from Judaism. The title of the book, which puts Jesus on the same level as Moses and Muhammad, in itself suggests that there will probably not be any problem between Jews and Christians once the latter have admitted that Jesus is not the son of God. Levy's son-in-law Paul Hesse, however, who (as was typical) owned a small foundry for precious metals, had abandoned his belief. He left notebooks relating the discussions he had had during the First World War when, called up as an officer, he spent his lunch times discussing theology with priests. The manuscript begins with a very precise self-definition: 'I declared, to begin with, that I was of the Jewish race and a freethinker in belief.' The word 'race' had not yet assumed its fateful connotations. Its use could be justified by the fact that, in this typical French 'Israelite' family, there had not as yet been any mixed marriages. Not until 1929 did Paul Hesse's granddaughter marry the son of a Breton engineer, himself the son of a gatekeeper and the grandson of a peasant. From 1791 to 1929: 138 years between the emancipation of the Jews and the first mixed marriage, i.e. five to six generations. Given these facts, how can we fail to sense the incredible acceleration that followed the Second World War? The means of mass communication, the raising of the level of education and women's liberation led the Muslim populations of France into mixed marriages much more quickly.

The 2008–9 survey *Trajectoires et origines* shows that 44 per cent of the descendants of masculine immigrants of Algerian

---

[1] New edition published by Kessinger Publishing, 2010.

or Moroccan origin have a spouse who is neither an immigrant nor a descendant of immigrants. The rate rises to 60
per cent for those of Tunisian origin, falls to 42 per cent for
those of Turkish origin, rises back to 65 per cent for those of
sub-Saharan African origin (we cannot, in this latter case, distinguish between Muslims and non-Muslims). For women,
the rates are a little lower, which is to be expected in disintegrating patrilineal cultures, but they remain at a very high
level for those of Algerian (41 per cent), Moroccan (34 per
cent), Tunisian (38 per cent) and sub-Saharan African (49
per cent) origin.[1] Only the rate of women of Turkish origin
is really low, at 7 per cent. These figures do not mean that all
is the best in the best of all possible worlds – far from it. But
while exogamy is not yet a majority practice, these groups
have clearly been welded to French society. And in no case
can these figures be read as suggesting that there is a 'Muslim
problem'. We need at this point to emphasize the speed with
which populations from sub-Saharan Africa have integrated –
and this says less about Africa than it does about France: the
host population really has no issues with skin colour.

There is, however, a 'Turkish problem' that, sadly, is
perhaps just a German problem. I examined this point in *Le
Destin des immigrés*. The resistance of Turkish populations to
assimilation was then even more obvious, though there was
nothing in their anthropological structure that could explain
it. Whatever the region of origin in Turkey, the rate of marriage between cousins was lower there than in North Africa.
Sometimes, this lower rate of family endogamy was linked
to a noticeably higher status for women. I noted the geographical distribution of Turkish immigration into France,
which stuck closely to the country's eastern border, and con-
cluded that the Turks of France were just a fragment of a

---

[1] *Immigrés et descendants d'immigrés en France*, p. 131.

more general immigration centred on Germany, an immigration that had interiorized on a European scale, both in France and in Belgium and the Netherlands, the norms of segregation that were effective on the other side of the Rhine. The rates of mixed marriage with Muslims were, at the time, insignificant in the Federal Republic of Germany. In France, at present, the rather high rate of mixed marriage among men of Turkish origin doubtless represents the first stage in a departure from the 'German model' in this population. We again come up against the fact that the epicentre of European differentialism is not located in France, but further to the north or east in Europe. This is why every step forward in the building of Europe will in the final analysis turn out to be a step forward in Islamophobia.

Ideologues and exogamy

So what is the truth about 'integration'? All the surveys tell us that integration is under way, that it has speeded up in comparison with the pre-war period, but has suddenly slowed down in recent times. Be this as it may, it leads to a disintegration in family structures and entails huge psychological pressures. And it is easy to see that economic stagnation is responsible for the current difficulties: there is no particular 'will' to survive that is responsible for the pause that is being registered at present. But at the current stage of rapidly rising Islamophobia, it is no longer enough to establish the truth of sociological facts. Bad faith itself needs to be detected. Young people of Muslim origin have been subjected to so many ideologically motivated trials and sentences that it seems necessary and fair to wonder whether they are really any less integrated than some of their judges.

These days, people sometimes refer to a 'Zemmourization'

of society, transforming the bearer of this patronym into a cultural icon. Let us take the anthropological approach to its logical conclusion and apply to Éric Zemmour the usual criteria for assessing the degree of assimilation. To do this, we can draw on the technique developed by the IFOP in a very fine study of the political corruption of the city of Perpignan: this study assesses the Muslim vote by the geographical distribution of patronyms from North Africa.[1] I am sure that Zemmour, who is well versed in political incorrectness, will not hold it against us if we note that his wife's maiden name suggests that he himself was perfectly happy to go for an endogamous marriage, in his community of origin (a Jewish community from North Africa), while he was himself born in Montreuil. So the Grand Inquisitor of young people of North African origin is less advanced in his assimilation than half of the *beurs* of Algerian origin who live in mixed couples. His typically Mediterranean prophetic utterances on masculinity complete the picture. Transcultural psychiatry would doubtless place him in the category of 'poorly assimilated North African'. But let us stick to a sociological approach. The central place occupied by Zemmour in the cultural landscape suggests that transcultural psychiatry would have plenty to say about the state of mind of the French middle classes.

Let us take a detour through the French Academy, where an electoral body with an average age of 78 has just elected Alain Finkielkraut, thus giving us the additional example of an ideologue, himself a Jew of Polish origin who is always ready to detect the 'Arab' or 'Black' dimension in France's social problems: he, too, has declined to take the leap into

---

[1] Jérôme Fourquet, Nicolas Lebourg and Sylvain Manternach, *Perpignan, une ville avant le Front national* (Paris: Fondation Jean-Jaurès, 2014).

mixed marriage, unlike so many young people of Algerian, Moroccan, Tunisian or Black African origin.

Of course, mixed marriage is not obligatory for anyone who wants to be a good French person. My Jewish forebears did their duty between 1914 and 1918 without previously having contracted the least mixed marriage. My grandmother made me laugh when she emphasized that the family's war correspondence, with letters being exchanged between one trench and another, was conducted solely between people called Alphen, Hesse, Levy, Strauss, Bloch and Worms. But please, please can endogamous ideologues stop giving lessons in Frenchness to the children of exogamous immigrants! Let us renew our link with France, a country that we have loved, a country that benevolently accepts the endogamy of those who prefer it, though she points out, discreetly and without any direct pressure, that it is after all by producing children from mixed origins that, in the historical long term, the national community can become an enduring entity.

The crushing of young people and the jihad factory

Before analysing how France – like Britain, Belgium and Denmark – manufactures jihadists for Islamic State, we should note, in the same spirit of equity, how the managing of affairs of Syria has revealed the incompetence of our rulers. Month after month, Laurent Fabius, *Le Monde* and a few others tried to commit France to military intervention against the Syrian regime. Our government noisily supported the forces that eventually created Islamic State. So, for a while, the movements of apprentice jihadists and of the French state followed parallel courses. And yet we have still not heard the least word of self-criticism on the part of the

French government for its past indulgence towards the most dangerous form of Islamism. Why should this surprise us? If the Minister of the Interior, Bernard Cazeneuve, has been exonerated of any responsibility for the failure to protect *Charlie Hebdo*, why would the mistakes made by Laurent Fabius, the Foreign Minister, be punished? If Cazeneuve can, in Copenhagen, in February 2015, openly state his support for the Danish police, Fabius certainly has the right to carry on travelling.

As we embark on an analysis of jihadism, we need to remain faithful to the method applied throughout this book: we must not jump on Islam as the cause of all our ills and on Muslims as the guilty party, but we should try to take apart the *French* social machinery (and that of the West as a whole) that leads young French people (or Westerners) to terrorism. The number of jihadist candidates – around a thousand at the beginning of 2015 – forces us to adopt this sociological treatment of the problem. The presence among them of a significant proportion of converts of Christian origin – 20 per cent, according to some statements from the Ministry of the Interior at the end of February 2015 – suggests, too, that we treat the problem of young people at the most general level.

One of the characteristics shared by all advanced societies is the economic and social crushing of their young people. Globalization, and free trade first and foremost, encourages this. The most orthodox theory provides the explanation. To show the extent to which the problem had arisen *before* the emergence of jihadism, let me quote from my own preface to the later edition of *L'Illusion économique*, a passage written in 1999:

> Liberal economic analysis also explains very clearly how, if not why, the young people of the Western world are being exploited. Globalization unifies labour markets. On the

global level, including the Third World, there is a relatively high number of young people willing to work hard, and the old people are fewer in number: they possess capital. The law of the equalization of the cost of factors assures us that if a developed country opens up to free trade, the most abundant factor, in this case capital, demographically identifiable with old people, will be favoured, and the relatively rare factor, labour, demographically identifiable with young people, will be placed at a disadvantage. This is exactly what we are experiencing: the crushing of young people, and of their freedom of work, of consumption and of movement, by free trade. Only a small percentage of young graduates from the most prestigious institutions are really safe from this mechanism of impoverishment.[1]

Of course, the euro aggravates the effects of free trade in its own zone. It is a strong, stable currency, managed with a view solely to keeping inflation low. The deflation on which we have now embarked will continue to privilege those who have fixed and guaranteed incomes, namely pensioners.

The aging of Western populations is producing elderly electorates in all places, and their preferences guide political decisions. Free trade was one of these choices – as was the priority given to ensuring pensions, by definition a measure that favours the elderly. To ensure material well-being, the combination 'guaranteed pension/free trade', i.e. 'guaranteed income/lower price of consumer goods', cannot be beaten: it has so far ensured a rise in the median income of the oldest citizens and a drop in that of the youngest, in the United States as in the United Kingdom and France. Here, there is

---

[1] Emmanuel Todd, *L'Illusion économique* (Paris: Gallimard, 'Folio' edn, 1999), pp. x–xii.

no opposition between the market, which ensures the compression of prices, and the state, which protects incomes.

The electorate, with a median age of 50, is definitely not what it was at 35. Democracy is changing in nature: it is getting stiff in the joints. The suicide rate among the over-65s is falling and there is a crisis brewing for political philosophy, which is going to have to approach the nature of the citizen in a more concrete and more physiological way.

We are forced to acknowledge at this point that the situation of the middle classes has found definite support in the existence of older generations whose economic interests chime in, for the time being, with those of executives and college graduates, even if they themselves are, generally speaking, neither very well educated nor very wealthy. The memory of the post-war years – a world without toilets, without bathrooms, without refrigerators, without televisions, without cars – is enough for today's elderly to appreciate their current situation at its worth, and side with the beneficiaries of the 'social state'.

Economic oppression is, of course, differential, and especially affects young people of Muslim origin: each family, placed within its particular social network, strives to protect its own children, and succeeds in doing so the more it is integrated into the French social fabric. In this survival game, it is inevitable that the last ones to have arrived are the least efficient: this is why we can to a large extent explain the higher level of unemployment among the children of immigrants without resorting to the hypothesis of discrimination. Islamophobia is just an aggravating factor. The very short period of time in which their lineage has been integrated into French society is the reason for a great deal of the higher rate of unemployment among young people of North African origin.

However, this does not mean that the oppression of young

people can be reduced to its economic dimension. Once we look beyond the cult of youth of Canal+, what we see on afternoon television is a series of adverts for accident-proof bathtubs, incontinence pads and funeral insurance. We live in a world ideologically dominated by age, in which young people are encouraged to think about their retirement even before they have found a job. Far from having elderly people who have stayed young at heart, the most advanced societies are manufacturing young people who are programmed for aging: for example, they want to buy somewhere to live as soon as possible – it will supplement their retirement – and thereby contribute, by making prices rise, to lessening the surface area they themselves can live in. To complete the picture, we need add only that 'the social state of the middle classes and the elderly' is not really investing any more in building new housing.

And if young people are not happy, they just have to go somewhere else: to America or Australia, anywhere so long as it is not in France. The possibility of travel and emigration for young people is one of the favourite themes in the media, especially the newspapers and magazines that are bought and read by the elderly. You can be a student or a chef in the United States, get bar work in London, or help out with humanitarian projects in West Africa: all adventures are ripe for the plucking. So why not be a jihadi fighter in Syria if you are one of the young people from the suburbs, stuck in a cycle of unemployment and petty delinquency? I am not joking. It can be claimed, quite seriously, that the mirage of Islamic State is merely an adaptation of the ideal of emigration for young people so warmly recommended by our magazines. According to the IFOP, in March 2014, 49 per cent of readers of *L'Express*, 56 per cent of readers of *Le Point*, and 57 per cent of readers of *Le Nouvel Observateur* were over the age of 50.

Without succumbing to reactionary, religious-type moralizing, we have to admit that the social and moral possibilities that are on offer to the young people of the most advanced societies are frankly inadequate, for all the technological progress around – which is indeed amazing and even intoxicating. But the prospect that faces young people after adolescence in France these days is not just one of video games, social media and a free-and-easy sexuality. It is also the *morally degrading* spectacle of a rising inequality and 10 per cent unemployment rate that are accepted as the norm; it is the permanent media circus of politicos pretending to be different from one other, and a Parliament already reduced to a theatre stage; it is the insensitivity of the pampered middle classes whose lives are depicted on television in the most enticing colours.

During this time, as we have seen, the prisons are filling, with young people (inevitably), and, needless to say, those who are of recent immigrant origin are overrepresented there. In France, furthermore, the state refuses to invest the money that is absolutely necessary for the prisoners to be given decent conditions, and the overpopulation of our jails adds to the harmful atmosphere of the prison environment. Prison radicalizes everything: petty delinquents become hardened criminals, and ordinary Muslims with traditional beliefs end up as terrorists. We are starting to understand which mechanisms turn a fantastical, deformed version of Islam into a reason for living and dying for so many young people, whether Muslim or not, and whether or not they have spent time in jail. And yet we should not forget that the alienation – and the exasperation – of young people can find other outlets in other parts of the Western world.

Scottish fundamentalism

We saw David Cameron, the British Prime Minister, strutting at the head of the 11 January demonstration as the financial press hailed the 'success' of his policies. But these policies are in actual fact just as austere as those of the Eurozone, and just as unable to reverse the drop in median income, especially of young people who are often forced to return to their parents' home after their studies, which completely flies in the face of the code of the nuclear family that demands they be autonomous. In France we have the ridiculous situation of a shrunken ruling class, often petty bourgeois but educated at the elite École nationale d'administration, while in England there is the even more ridiculous situation of a ruling caste selected to rule right from the moment it goes to secondary school – a coterie of former pupils from a handful of ruinously expensive private schools, Eton first and foremost.

However many immigrants of Pakistani origin there may be in Glasgow and Edinburgh, the contribution made by Scotland to jihad will probably remain modest. But thanks to his blind support for the values of his time (especially the values of the stock exchange), David Cameron has led the young people of Scotland towards secession. In the referendum of September 2014, 57 per cent of Scots aged between 16 and 34 voted for independence; 73 per cent of the over-65s voted to stay in the Union. For anyone who is familiar with the history of the United Kingdom, this threat of endogenous dissolution, made worse by the alienation of young people, is just as alarming as, although less violent than, the jihadism found in the suburbs of France. After all, the 1707 Act of Union, which brought together the parliaments of the two nations, did trigger a period of extraordinary prosperity in Scotland. The contribution of this small northern nation to the intellectual and scientific history of Great Britain was huge, exemplified by David Hume, Adam Ferguson, Adam Smith, James Watt, James Clark Maxwell, Lord Kelvin and others. It has been rare for two nations to be melded together so successfully. Thanks to the United Kingdom, Scotland was one of the leading countries of modernity. So the alienation of its young people is proof that everywhere, absolutely everywhere, at different speeds and in various forms, the question of the intrinsic staying power of Western societies is going to raise its head. All forms of dissidence can henceforth be imagined.

The problems of national cohesion that are looming in France will not be purely 'Muslim', or even purely religious. While there is still time, we need to think of Brittany, which has been neglected, and Alsace, mistreated by the territorial reforms. When people demonstrated in western Brittany in the autumn of 2014, wearing the red bonnets of the great tax revolt of 1675, this was doubtless just a warning, given for free, of their desire for greater autonomy.

Moving beyond the fear of religion

At this stage, we need to make an effort to try to understand why Islam, a religion introduced into France (and other countries) by minority groups that are generally rather poor and of low social standing, is seducing young people, some of whom are embarking on what looks like a return to their religion of origin, while others, from a Catholic or secular background, are purely and simply changing religion.

We will not make much progress by hysterically denying any value to the religious sphere. What France, a country undergoing a metaphysical crisis, is most sorely lacking is a minimal ability to reflect serenely about what people can get out of religion. At the risk of annoying Charlie, who now identifies French national identity with the right to blaspheme against Muhammad, we need to think about what Islam can offer to some of the French. Basically, we need just to extend to other religious systems our earlier analysis of zombie Catholicism, which admitted not just the negative role of Catholicism in many areas, but also the positive role played by the spirit of cooperation that has sprung from Catholicism. We need to apply Polanyi to Islam as well as to Catholicism – not to Islam in general, but to the way it is, in France, supported by specific groups who actually practise their religion to a far lesser extent than is generally thought.

Furthermore, nothing justifies the idea that all religions, at all times, oppose progress. On the contrary: what is demonstrated by the cases of Protestantism and Judaism, two religions of the Book that have created peoples of a very high cultural level, is that in the development of societies, faith was a forerunner of mass education. The Protestant countries, especially those in Scandinavia, have been in the vanguard since the Reformation and they still have a very high level of education, as does the State of Israel. The presence of Finland at the top of the league table of educational surveys, such as PISA, which measure the performances of secondary school pupils, owes a great deal to Luther, very little to its government – and nothing at all to advanced capitalism. It is the best example of zombie Protestantism. The story has been very different in France, where the Church of belated and backward-looking Catholicism put a damper on the spread of literacy. This is probably the (unconscious) reason why most French people, prisoners of their own history, are nowadays unable to have any positive feelings about religion.

Quite apart from the debatable question of the existence of God and the plausibility of the conditions for gaining eternal life, the existence of an ideal combining an individual ethic, a collective project and a future that might be filled with beauty can help human beings in their attempts to become something other than vulnerable animals released into a world deprived of meaning. This is why we need to envisage the possibility of Islam making a positive contribution, in certain circumstances and in some of its varieties, to the psychological equilibrium of individuals, to good results at school and a successful integration into French society. We are not thinking here of using Islam to restructure the suburbs, of course! But we need to be fully aware that it is anomie, much more than communitarianism, that poses a threat to life in our towns and cities. The assimilation of French family values and ideology is far too advanced here. But what we *can* imagine is a contribution on the margins of Muslim belief, one that would be of importance for some families engaged in the attempt to improve their children's intellectual, educational and social lot. They would just need to be left alone – or, even better, to be protected against the insults and attacks of militant atheism, against the new threat to the liberty of belief that is constituted nowadays by *radical secularism*. This new type of faith needs to be kept outside state schools just as much as Catholicism, Protestantism, Judaism and Islam.

Islam and equality

The real question that Islam raises for French society is not just the way that, as an ancient form of worship in a metaphysically empty world, it presents itself as a substitute. It has already lost the strength to do that. The populations that transmitted Islam originally are undergoing secularization, like the others, albeit a little later. But Islam, like Catholicism and Protestantism, is able to transmit values to a population that has lost its beliefs, and to remain active even after it has vanished as a living faith. We have been obliged to admit that there is a zombie Catholicism, and a zombie

Protestantism too. We should not shy away from postulating that there is a zombie Islam. Now what is specific about Islam is a powerful sense of the equality of all human beings. The traditional Arab family defines brothers as equal, as do the ideal rules of inheritance set out in the Quran. I will discuss the question of the 'disadvantaging of women' later. The father's weak authority is combined with the equality of brothers to produce the central characteristic of the largely horizontal organization of the Arab family, namely the solidarity of brothers.

Some of Islam's powers of expansion, indeed, come from the way it is basically egalitarian, both in its scriptures and in the family structures that have kept it going. In the case of France, the egalitarianism of Islam, currently perceived as a threat, could become a real opportunity.

The political behaviour of populations of Muslim origin in France shows a strong tendency to vote on the left. Given their class composition and the ideological attacks to which they have been exposed for many years, it is only to be expected that electors of Muslim origin will vote this way, even though the French left is at present more than suspect, as we have seen, in its deepest values. The fact remains that the strength of this left-voting tendency, as measured by IFOP surveys, leads us to conclude that an intrinsic ideological dynamic is at work here. For 80 per cent of 'French Muslims' consistently vote on the left.

If we put aside the period of the anti-Sarkozy 'emergency' of 2007, the strength of the vote for the far left is especially remarkable. If all French manual workers were Muslims, Jean-Luc Mélenchon would have real political clout.

And yet, how can we describe as egalitarian a religion and a family organization that consign women to such a low status? This is the question raised by some people – but it stems from a naive and ahistorical view of the notion of

Table 5.1 The evolution of the Muslim vote in the first round of the presidential elections in 2002, 2007 and 2012[1]

	Presidential elections 2002	Presidential elections 2007	Presidential elections 2012
Far left Communist Party	19	10	21
Socialist Party + allies	49	58	57
Greens	11	3	2
Bayrou	2	15	6
Right	17	8	7
Boutin/Villiers/ Dupont-Aignan	1	2	2
Far right	1	1	4
Others	–	3	1

[1] IFOP, Focus no. 88, 2013.

equality, particularly when we are talking of equality within family structures.

The inequality of the sexes

It is true that, in the Paris Basin, the egalitarian nuclear family defines all children, whether sons or daughters, as equal when it comes to inheritance. So it is natural for a French person to think that equality between men, on the one hand, and between women and men, on the other, are merely the application of one and the same principle. This is not the case generally speaking. In Anglo-American and Scandinavian countries, for example, the elevated status of women is combined with an absence of a principle of equality between men – in a context of family and inheritance, between boys. The egalitarian nuclear family of the Paris Basin is the outcome of a long history, which itself is the result of the history of the egalitarian nuclear family of the Late Roman Empire, which already treated children of both sexes as equals. But if we go even further back, there had been the family of republican Rome: this considered only boys to be symmetrical. At the origin of the principle of family equality we always find – in China, in Northern India, in Russia – a patrilineal organization that *defines men as equal in opposition to women.* This is the case of the Arab family.

The Arab endogamous communitarian family, built around principles of equality and solidarity between brothers, defines a universalism restricted to men. The psychological mechanism is of the usual type: 'If brothers are equal, men are equal, peoples are equal, but with this reservation: women are not men.'

So Islam is universalist, like the French Revolution or Russian Communism, or indeed the Christianity of the Roman Empire. This is the main reason why this religion tends these days to express, across the world, a vague aspiration towards equality, that equality that has been so mistreated by economic globalization. The lessening of France's influence in the world, as well as the collapse of communism, have created a vacuum at the heart of the global system of representation of values, even if Russia, back on its feet but less powerful than it once was, is endeavouring to reassume its place as the official representative of the equality of peoples and nations in the geopolitical concert.

But anthropology will here rid us of the intuitively reasonable idea that there is just one form of universalism. Anthropology demonstrates that the principle of the universal human being is rooted in specific family systems, and that

French, Russian and Arab universalisms are in actual fact just particular variants.

The way Islam represents the value of equality is a problem, because it clearly excludes women. To be sure, Youssef Courbage and I showed, in our *A Convergence of Civilizations*, that the demographic evolution of the Arab world presupposed a rapid rise in the status of women. But it will be a long time before it converges with Western Europe.[1] The anthropological distance remains significant. It is clear that egalitarian and universal values are common to those who, in Europe and the Arab world, are demanding equality of rights for the Palestinians. But we still need to bear in mind the (unpleasant) fact that, in the depths of anthropological systems, different conceptions of the status of women separate European and Muslim universalisms.

European universalism is rapidly declining, as a result of the implosion of French universalism and the rise of Germany. Muslim universalism is thriving, as the rise of literacy rates is ideologically invigorating the Arab world as a whole, which is egalitarian in the sphere of family values. The injustice perpetrated against the Palestinians does, of course, stir those remnants of the universal values of the Revolution that are still left in France, thereby triggering feelings of solidarity, but, all the same, in terms of lifestyle the French are closer to the Israelis. This basic contradiction is the reason why ideological interactions between Europe and the Arab world always end up producing more confusion and violence than solutions and peace. The mirage of Islamic State has replaced the Palestinian mirage. It draws certain young people into senseless ventures. It also blinds analysts

---

[1] Emmanuel Todd and Youssef Courbage, *A Convergence of Civilizations. The Transformation of Muslim Societies around the World*, trans. George Holoch, Jr. (New York: Columbia University Press, 2011).

to the internal dynamics of French society. The anthropological conflict between the two universalisms — French and Arab — may remain insoluble for a few more years in the Middle East, but it is fading away quite naturally in France itself.

The *beurs* of the French suburbs are French and have already, in terms of their manners and customs, travelled the nine-tenths or even ten-tenths of the way to an egalitarian conception of the statuses of women and men. I have already had occasion to note that, by means of a mixed marriage, half the young people of Algerian origin were more advanced in assimilation than some theorists of the failure of integration. Once this element is factored into the argument, we can go much further. And rather than lamenting the failure of integration, we need to ask whether a zombie Islam might not contribute to a positive rebalancing of French political culture. For it is anthropologically perfectly clear that, once Islam has dissolved the antifeminist element of Arab culture, it is more than compatible with the egalitarianism of the Paris Basin or the Mediterranean seafront.

I have described French society as affected by inequality, a subjective value and an objective reality. I have shown how ideological and political power has been seized by regions and classes that are predisposed to inequality, namely zombie Catholic provinces and higher social strata. As a result, we are forced to accept that there has been a relative collapse in the egalitarian culture of *la France centrale*, the France that carried out the Revolution and ensured that a truly republican Republic could flourish. The main political agent of the subversion of national culture was the Socialist Party, a discreet but powerful agent of rising inegalitarianism.

With regard to equality, the Arab family and its Islam are closer to the tradition of *la France centrale* than are the zombie Catholic provinces and neo-republican ideology. We sensed as much in the high vote for the far left among French people of Muslim influence, which is very much in line with the traditional Communist vote of the 'red' suburbs. So an anthropologist is duty bound to emphasize that, insofar as it preserves some of its strength and its specific character, a transformed Arab and Muslim culture could well and truly contribute to the re-establishment of a veritable republicanism in France. This optimistic conclusion is obviously of the greatest importance, but we still need to take our argument to a logical conclusion, without leaving out the potentially dangerous elements of egalitarian culture, whether Muslim or republican.

The anti-Semitism of the suburbs

The previous chapter was mainly devoted to the perversion of lower-class egalitarianism in the heart of the republican middle. This egalitarianism takes the form of a vote for the National Front. I also referred to other perversions created by universalism, older perversions, first monarchical and then republican: the final rejection of the Protestants in 1685, the massacre of the Vendée counter-revolutionaries and the Anglophobia of 1793, the anti-Semitism of an egalitarian variety among those who settled in North Africa around 1898, and the Germanophobia of 1914. In 2015, we need to treat the latent anti-Semitism of some young people of North African origin with the same rigour. It is not difficult to identify the anti-Semitism of the suburbs as a new perversion of egalitarianism.

Merah, Nemmouche, Coulibaly: the anti-Jewish feelings that prosper in certain milieus are now explicit and completely undeniable, and need to be treated as a sociological fact, like the suicide rate. We would still be wrong to see

them as just a way of importing the Israeli–Palestinian conflict into France, even if the distant reality of the injustice
perpetrated on the Palestinians consciously motivates the
young anti-Semites of the suburbs. Lower-class, egalitarian
National Front voters have turned their resentment against
the visible difference of original Arab culture; likewise, some
descendants of immigrants who have been acculturated by
France are turning their resentment against the visible difference of practising Jews in the northeast of Paris and its
suburbs, and in various regions of the south of France. A
hysterical form of egalitarianism can lead, as we have just
seen, to a rejection of the other: the latter is perceived as
different when he or she should be similar, and is finally clas-
sified as 'non-human'.

In the case of the Paris region, it is in practice and in
theory quite impossible to distinguish, in the rejection of
the Jewish difference by many adolescents in the suburbs,
between what might be the product of the universalism of
the culture of *la France centrale* and what might come from a
persistence of Muslim universalism.

Nonetheless, there is a structural difference between
the Arabophobia of the National Front electorate and the
anti-Semitism of the suburbs. The National Front vote
also results from a mechanism of educative stratification
that leads the lower classes to seek a scapegoat in the social
hierarchy below them. In the case of the anti-Semitism of
the suburbs, young people cannot perceive practising Jews
as socially inferior. They are few in number, which admittedly makes them ideal scapegoats, but in the context of an
atomization of the surrounding social milieu, it is easier to
imagine that practising Jews are envied. Their membership
of a community means they are protected from the void that
stretches out across the periphery of French society.

The anthropological basis of the populations of North

African origin in the Paris region is egalitarian twice over, being both Parisian and Muslim; it melds together, in an unstable mixture, the regionally dominant individualism and the ongoing disintegration of the endogamous communitarian family; in reality, it deprives people of any collective protection. Individuals of North African origin are, like most French people in the Paris Basin, much more seriously threatened by anomie than by communitarianism. Conversely, Jewish culture, in itself differentialist, makes a withdrawal into the community effective should the need arise. The Jewish family insists on the closeness of brothers and cousins, but it does not include any principle of equality. The Bible stages a constant oscillation between a theoretical preference for the firstborn (Esau) and the actual choice of the son born last (Jacob).[1] It is strong on identity, and on education. The Jewish tradition is exogamous from the family point of view,[2] but it does not have, as Christian cultures do, an absolute phobia for marriages between cousins, which it tolerates when the small size of the group makes them necessary.

Still, irrespective of the all-too-obvious differences between the National Front vote and the anti-Semitism of the suburbs, we are in both cases faced with the alarming mechanism of a universalism that is being made racist by its temporary inability to assimilate or to dissolve. Higher up in the social structure, Charlie, borne by the rise in inequality, can happily go out and demonstrate, in the name of his higher values, and condemn the two lower-class, egalitarian and insecure groups, namely National Front voters (perceived as racist) and *beurs* (perceived as anti-Semitic).

---

[1] I have analysed the original Jewish family system in *L'Origine des systèmes familiaux* (Paris: Gallimard-Seuil, 2011), pp. 541–46.
[2] But endogamous, of course, from the community point of view.

And yet it is this smug, self-satisfied middle class that has, through its selfishness and disdain, allowed French society to decay in its lower strata, day by day without any end in sight, thereby condemning entire categories to a social marginalization in which they can brood at leisure over their rage and frustration. Never mind the antiracist professions of faith, or the government's solemn and repeated promises to fight anti-Semitism, the truth is that Charlie has managed, after a gigantic game of sociological billiards, to place French Jews in danger by mistreating French Muslims. And, as a result of its insensitive and cruel economic policies, it will obstinately continue to do so.

Conclusion

In this conclusion, I should like to give a brief overview of what the republican France of the past once was, and then summarize what the neo-republican France of the present has become, before finally stating the choice we are faced with: confrontation with Islam, or an accommodation with it. I will end with a sensibly pessimistic prediction on what threatens to happen.

The real republican past

In the wake of the Dreyfus Affair and the separation of Church and State, as I have said, the Third Republic was, in spite of its celebration of Jacobinism, actually a pluricultural place. I will refrain from using the term 'multiculturalism' here, as it is too marked by ideology and always masks a deeply rooted intolerance. Pluricultural is meant to refer to the complete opposite: an explicit intolerance that masks the liberty of all. At its heart, France was not religious. In a constellation of peripheral provinces, a third of the national territory, the Catholic Church reigned. It had its idols and its schools. The behaviour of Catholic populations was extremely deviant: people married late, couples rejected birth control, there were big families. Its birth rate, 25 per cent higher than elsewhere, could give the impression that the Church was seeking to conquer the Republic by demographic means. At the centre of the national culture, a relaxed attitude to sexuality predominated, quite unparalleled anywhere else in Europe. Members of the English, German and Italian aristocracy and bourgeoisie came to seek, and find, the conditions of their liberty in Paris.

Although secular culture and Catholic culture were officially at loggerheads, they were not hermetically sealed off from one another. Every day, Catholics defected and moved over to the side of free thought. There were many mixed marriages between the two camps – and these unions were usually favourable to the dominant central culture. Of course there were widespread tensions, but the Jewish and Protestant minorities had finally found liberty in this pluricultural world. This whimsical and disciplined France, anarchist at heart but authoritarian in its Church and its State, fascinated Europe, not only through its motto, 'Liberté, égalité, fraternité', but through its cultural diversity, greater than that of any other nation.

Let us hear what a brilliant geneticist, a caricature of the eccentric Englishman, J.B.S. Haldane had to say. He was on the far left; he did not think that human beings were equal, but this minor defect did allow him to see the France of the 1930s in its real place among the nations:

A young civilization tends to be less tolerant of diversity than an old. A violent and successful political or social change often standardizes admiration of a particular type. The Italian Fascist models himself on a certain strong, though by no means silent, man. The American, born aloft on an immense wave of commercial prosperity, idealizes the capitalists and inventors who have organized that prosperity. In certain stable communities a more tolerant attitude prevails. Under the third French Republic it is probable that more different human types are encouraged than in any other society. Let us take seven human beings who have achieved fame under it: Pasteur, Renan, Anatole France, Marshall Foch, Ste. Thérèse de l'Enfant Jesus, Sarah Bernhardt and Suzanne Lenglen. I doubt whether any other state could produce a team quite so thoroughly representative of the different sides of human nature. In England, for example, certain of Anatole France's works would have been suppressed on the ground of indecency, and Ste. Thérèse would have found considerable difficulty in being saintly when alive, and almost insuperable obstacles to performing well-attested miracles after her death.

It is unnecessary to add that France, in spite of this immense diversity of human types, possesses as characteristic a culture and as high a degree of national unity in times of crisis as any other state.[1]

In other terms, France's pluricultural character allowed individuals to flourish thanks to a process that Jacobin theory had not in the least anticipated. The secular homogeneity of the past is a complete fantasy. The theory put about these days by radical secularism is a pure fiction. *What is now being demanded of Muslims was never obtained from Catholics*, in spite

[1] *The Inequality of Man* (Harmondsworth: Penguin Books, 1937), pp. 47–48.

of more than one hundred years of violent conflict, including the 200,000 dead in the Vendée war.

The neo-republican present

Neo-republicanism is a strange doctrine, which claims to speak the language of Marianne but in actual fact defines a Republic of exclusion. Over the past thirty years, the rise of the zombie Catholic periphery in France and the crisis that has befallen the secular centre, both combined together, have led to a sudden dramatic shift: now it is the periphery that is the dominant party, and with it, its indifference towards or even its rejection of the value of equality. The regions that supported the monarchy, and the conservative right too, followed by Vichy, are in charge. And France as an organized system has changed its nature.

The culture of *la France centrale* is disorganized. It has not vanished, of course, and probably still has a strong latent potential, active beneath the surface, but its effective contribution to the national system mainly finds an echo, in traditional lower-class milieus and among the descendants of Muslim immigrants, as the expression of a specific egalitarian intolerance, a perversion of universalism which, of course, makes things even worse. The duality of the national system no longer ensures, as it did when Haldane was writing, a maximum diversity of human possibilities. Quite the opposite: it increases the anxiety that is bred on a massive scale by the atomization of the central system. Anomie, a hybrid and unstable intolerance combining egalitarianism with inegalitarianism: this is what has led to the rise of Islamophobia as a national factor to be counted with. Irrespective of any problem of adaptation of populations of which it is the religion of origin, Islam is indeed the scapegoat of a society that no longer knows what to do with its lack of belief and no longer knows whether it has faith in equality or inequality. What has emerged from this confusion is neo-republican discourse, which demands secularism and unanimity. The ubiquitous words 'secular' and 'Republic', over the past twenty years, also reveal the decline of any real republican feeling. As often happens, the truth advances wearing a mask – the mask of its own denial.

The neo-Republic, closer in concept to Vichy than to the Third Republic, demands from some of its citizens an intolerable degree of renunciation to what they are. In order to be recognized as good French men and women, Muslims are forced to accept that it is a good thing to blaspheme against their own religion. And this comes down to asking them, in actual fact, to stop being Muslims. Bestselling ideologues mention deportation as a solution.

Like Vichy, the neo-Republic is not an independent national system. It is just one part of a complex multinational system, Europe, or rather, as Valéry Giscard d'Estaing quite frankly suggests by his choice of title for one of his books, *Europa*. Europa is not an association of free and equal nations, the extension of a French conception to the whole continent. Europa is a hierarchical system dominated by one nation, Germany, while the others line up along a finely graduated scale, from the voluntary servitude of France to the servitude *tout court* of South European countries. The existence of Europa turned the great demonstration of 11 January into a regional phenomenon, which deployed itself in one of the system's provinces. But the centre of gravity of Islamophobia is elsewhere, and falls into two geographically separate circles.

The Islamophobic dynamic is partly characteristic of the Eurozone as a whole, which itself is structured by its zombie Catholic provinces with their inegalitarian temperament.

This type C (as in Catholic) Islamophobia is to some extent moderated by a residue of the universal sentiment inherited from the Church, but it tends to be affected by the failure of the euro, which makes the upper strata anxious and pushes them towards the pursuit of a scapegoat – Islam, of course. The ruling classes of the Eurozone would probably have preferred Russophobia, the ideal xenophobia of the elites. But the Russians lack two features essential to a satisfactory scapegoat: a significant physical presence in the West and, above all, weakness. Beating up immigrants from the Mediterranean seems less risky, when all is said and done, than confronting the Russian army.

The second circle, that of type P (as in Protestant) Islamophobia is situated further north and does not coincide with the Eurozone. But while Protestantism may have bequeathed its educational dynamism to its zombie offspring, it has also passed on its basically negative relation to the universal. For quite some time, zombie Protestantism has been acting in Europe – in the Netherlands, in Denmark, in North and East Germany – as a catalyst of Islamophobia.

The neo-republican system is dominated by middle classes that are so far not suffering too much from the crisis in the economic system. They have taken over control of the French social state and have agreed to sacrifice industry and the world of the working class. They are anxious, and show signs of ideological instability. It is easy to detect the gradual rise of Islamophobia within them. Muslims, a fantasy category, are thus becoming a second problem in their view, next to the lower classes. Their good conscience is now obliged to fight a war on two fronts: against both populism and against Islamism.

Charlie has just shown how able he is to protect his way of life and his beliefs. The great neo-republican demonstrations of 11 January were marked by hysteria, by densification and also by expansion, as a reconquest of the lower-middle classes was on this occasion brought about. The emotional shock resulting from the horror of 7 January presented the possibility of a reaffirmation of the ideology dominating France: free trade, the social state, pro-Europeanism and austerity. What is new, and really disturbing, is the obsession with Islam, the frenzied secular discourse that is spreading throughout the upper half of the social pyramid and is much more alarming, basically, than the way that the National Front vote is taking root in the lower classes.

Dramatic revolutionary shifts, whether to the left or the right, always result from movements of opinion among the middle classes, not within the proletariat, who only ever act as a 'mass for manoeuvre'. The Marxist tradition has often mocked the petty bourgeoisie. But it is the petty bourgeoisie, and not the proletariat, that makes history: the French Revolution, Fascism, Nazism, and even Communism, since the Bolshevik Party was actually the creation of a petty bourgeois intelligentsia. The placidity of the English and American middle classes is what lies behind the stability of liberal democracy in Great Britain and the United States.

As I have suggested, France is now faced with a choice between two options.

Future 1: confrontation

If France continues along the path of a confrontation with Islam, it needs, quite simply, to retrench and split. Among the younger generations, the French people who are classed as 'Muslims' comprise some 10 per cent of the population. So France is hardly being swamped by Muslims in the way that radical secularists claim, since the majority of these 'Muslims' do not in fact practise their religion all that much;

many of them are married to French people of more ancient origin. But there are now Muslims everywhere, at every level of French society, and a good number of them are welded to the central body of French society by their ancestry. So any intensification of the struggle against Islam can in no way lead to its being vanquished. What it will do is alienate the completely assimilated Muslims. It will harden the protective beliefs of the peaceful Muslims of the French suburbs and provinces. In conditions of endless unemployment, under the dark skies of a Europe that worships the golden calf, in the absence of any future they can relate to, it is more or less certain that an increasing number will go over to radical Islamism. Conversions to Islam among young people of European origin ought to be most frequent in that part of French territory whose anthropological backdrop is nuclear and individualist, i.e. in a vast Paris Basin area – in Normandy, Picardy, Champagne, Touraine and Burgundy – since this is where the generations have less solidarity with each other and the young people feel the most abandoned.

We need to realize that if a proportion of young people are deprived of 'meaning', of the 'religious' dimension, any additional targeting of Islam as a guilty party will merely turn it into an ideal escape route. What appears as a terrible problem in the eyes of the older generation will appear to be a solution to the young. Trying to indoctrinate school children in secularism, that new religion, and militarizing the students and unemployed by civic service, filling the prisons with young kids, keeping tabs on them when they are released – all of this will merely worsen the situation if Islam is indeed becoming an escape from the nightmare experienced by young people who do not know which way to turn.

But France simply does not have the means to stage such a confrontation. It survived the expulsion of the Protestants and the Vendée war only because it was then the main European power in demographic terms. But it is clear that, at present, reducing 10 per cent of its young population to the status of second-class citizens and the flight to the Anglo-American world of the most gifted among them would spell out the end of France as a medium power.

In any case, when racism takes hold of people's minds, it never stops at this or that category. Confrontation with Islam has already triggered a resurgence of anti-Semitism. I doubt whether the spread of this anti-Semitism, in a society obsessed with religion and economically stagnant, will stop at the gates of Paris and the main cities of France. The middle classes will very soon be affected by an infiltration of bad feelings, which will need just to reactivate the old Catholic anti-Semitism and serve it up in a new zombie version. Then the Jews will leave too, more quickly and in greater numbers than the Muslims. I would be surprised if such a nation would still be as alluring to its citizens of Asian origin. Some French people of Chinese origin will also start leaving France, doubtless for the United States.

Do those ideologues who recommend that we stay firm and go for homogeneity even realize that France can remain a real European power thanks to its diversity? In France, there are more citizens of Muslim, African, Jewish and Chinese origin than in any other European nation. It is thanks to them that Paris is a world city.

I am also convinced that the emergence of an Islamophobic France, abandoned by its most dynamic minorities, would end up seeming tiresome to even some of its own provinces. I have already mentioned Brittany and Alsace. But what would an extended Rhône-Alpes region do in this case? It is also a zombie Catholic area, where it is easy to sense already, in the east, the economic and political effects of the European gravitational field.

One of the particularities of the Western world in its current crisis is a collective variety of narcissism, without any doubt an aggregation of the individual narcissisms that are part of the spirit of the age. Its overall system and its national subsystems, like its individuals, think themselves admired by the whole world, the focus of everyone's attention. This narcissistic West perceives Moscow as 'isolated from the international community' at the very same time as the Central Bank of China is saving the rouble, Turkey is offering itself to Russia as a transit country for the South Stream pipeline blocked by Europe in Bulgaria, and Iran and India are buying up huge quantities of Russian military materiel. As if NATO were not already quite ridiculous enough.

But the France of François Hollande is currently affected by a narcissistic vertigo of the first magnitude. On 11 January 2015, the president proclaimed Paris to be the capital of the world. It is true that, in the wake of the attacks, France did benefit from a huge wave of sympathy. That moment has passed. The publication of the survivors' issue of *Charlie Hebdo* dated 14 January 2015, which again struck out at Muhammad, led to a moral isolation of France unprecedented in history. True, France can count on Denmark, its master in caricature; on Germany, the theorist of circumcision; on the Netherlands, a country that has sadly shown the way when it comes to Islamophobic personalities being assassinated – but on who else?

The Anglo-American press refused to reproduce the *Charlie* of 14 January 2015. The Russians, the Japanese, the Chinese and the Indians all thought that France was being pointlessly insulting – badly brought up, in a word. I almost forgot to mention the Muslim world as a whole. The fact of the matter is that, locked in our radical secularism, we French find ourselves alone, tragically provincial, like some ethnic gang bowing down to its idol amid general indifference or disapproval. In the age of globalization, you do not insult the cultural symbols of other people just for 'fun'.

The elites from religious minorities of foreign origin will take flight; the provinces will defect; France will be morally isolated in a globalized world. Yes, the end of France is a not unthinkable prospect. And this will not be the fault of Islam, but of Islamophobes.

Future 2: the return to the Republic: an accommodation with Islam

This scenario would, of course, be meaningful only in the context of a regained national liberty. Unless France leaves the euro, no economic policy will be possible, no lowering of unemployment, no conceivable improvement in the situation of those who are economically the most vulnerable – the young, whether of Muslim origin or not. Pro-Europeanism and Islamophobia are now inextricably linked. Symmetrically, keeping Islamophobia and anti-Semitism at bay is unthinkable unless France exits from the quagmire of pro-European sentiment.

To avoid any misunderstanding, the kernel of the republican pact should be remembered, before we examine the option of an accommodation with Islam. This sets out what the Republic must unflinchingly maintain.

1 *On the right to blasphemy*
   (a) The right to blasphemy is absolute. The police must ensure the physical safety of blasphemers. Ministers of the Interior who fail in this task must explain themselves to the nation.
   (b) French citizens, whether Muslim or not, who consider

that it is pointless and cowardly to blaspheme against the religion of a dominated group, have the right to say so without being accused either of being apologists for terrorism, or of not being good French citizens. The state must protect their freedom of expression.

2   *On assimilation as a necessary horizon*
   (a) It is the destiny of French people of all origins to live together as free and equal individuals: this will imply, in a future that does not need to be specified, the gradual fusion of groups by the spontaneous increase in the number of mixed marriages.
   (b) The mixing of populations presupposes the fading away of religious differences and, it must be admitted, a predominance of religious scepticism and free thought.
   (c) The equality in status of women and men is a precondition of mixed marriages. In the territory of the Republic, this must be an article of faith. Only a convergence of views on what a couple needs to be can authorize marriage between individuals of different origins. Thus, the banning of the Islamic headscarf in schools, which symbolizes the equality of women and the French demand for exogamy, is a good thing. It was a positive step, and is still necessary.

In this way, I am still an assimilationist. But I also persist in thinking that the secular discourse is ignorant, or in bad faith, when it links the low status of women to Muslim theology, when it states that the civil legislation contained in the Quran seriously contradicts the French *code civil*. For *Islam always accepts the priority of local usage over the sacred text. Nowhere in the Muslim world are the rules of inheritance contained in the Quran applied.* The notorious 'half share' for girls is not granted by the peasants of the Arab world. Conversely, and in complete freedom from Muhammad's message, the most oriental version of Islam gives girls the advantage over boys. Beyond the Indian Ocean, indeed, Islam places women at the heart of the family structure. Indonesia, the most populous of all Muslim countries, is mainly matrilocal, and its most practising ethnic groups, such as the Minangkabaus, are frankly matrilineal. Sometimes, indeed, this can give rise to difficulties for men. An egalitarian Islam, from the point of view of relations between the sexes, already exists: it is the daily experience of 250 million Indonesians.

Envisaging assimilation as the sole solution should not lead to any dogmatic and counterproductive application of principles. The dream needs to face up to the reality of the world, the rhythms of life, the social and economic difficulties of the time. The ideology of the universal human being should, from this point of view, lead neither the citizen of the host country nor the immigrant to cease being a human being. We need to give time to time – accept that we have to live through imperfect transitional moments, to be gentle with each other's weaknesses. Not just because such an attitude is good in itself – and it really is – but also because kindliness is in the long term more effective than confrontation, which always generates hatred and polarization.

The assimilation of the children of Muslim origin is already well advanced, but is currently being slowed down by economic difficulties, by the uncertainty in French society itself about its own goals. The atomization and emptiness that accompany or, more precisely, characterize the crisis in the developed world mean that everywhere mechanisms of sheltering, of communitarianism, are being set in motion: they are probably stronger in the France of zombie Catholicism and certain fractions of the Jewish population than in the population of Muslim origin, where family structures are disintegrating. In a context like this, France cannot forbid its Muslim citizens to practise their religion freely and to say, if they believe it to be so, that the caricatures of Muhammad are obscene. This is just a very small part of the problem. Islam needs finally to be generally accepted, legitimated as a component of the nation, just as the Church was. We need to accept the free building of mosques – indeed, we need to make up for our backwardness in this area.

What has just been described is no utopia. *It is the demand for a return to the true past of the Republic. We need to grant to Islam what was granted to Catholicism*, in the era of triumphant secularism. The modest size and the fragmentation of the population of Muslim origin in the suburbs mean we cannot draw too close a parallel with the provinces of the Catholic periphery. A 5–10 per cent Muslim population, depending on whether we are looking at the old or the young, dispersed groups that are varied in nationality of origin and religious practice, will never weigh as much in the balance as the third of those provinces that were Catholic, which were in their day much more homogenous and much better stocked with members of the middle and ruling classes. The Islam of the future will be, in terms of power, between a third and a twentieth part of what the Church represented in the Republic.

Finally, we need, out of realism and necessity, to admit fully and joyfully that there is now, in French culture, in our national being, a Muslim province. We also need to avoid a new Vendée war, that confrontation which contributed to solidifying Catholicism. It was an accepted Catholicism that spontaneously dissolved in the wake of the Second World War. Our new province, Islam, believes in equality, unlike the Church, which is based on a principle of hierarchy that flies in the face of the republican ideal in every point. Thus, a positive integration of Islam would help to reinforce republican culture rather than subverting it.

We need to wait for time, rather than ideology, to attenuate the tensions: more peaceful human relations will lead to a greater degree of religious relativism, even more mixed marriages and ever more French people who are unable to describe their beliefs and their religious origins in any simple way.

Admittedly, the resumption of a faster speed of assimilation of the populations concerned cannot be counted on, given the emptiness, in Polanyi's sense of the term, generated by advanced capitalism. But accommodation can work where confrontation will only fail. The truth is that *any level of probability of accommodation succeeding is acceptable*, as the probability of confrontation failing is 100 per cent.

A foreseeable deterioration

Confrontation, acceptance: both options exist, but we have to admit that French society has today embarked on the road to confrontation. Charlie's selfish complacency, the votes for the National Front, the anti-Semitism of the suburbs, all lead one to doubt whether a change of direction might be possible.

What France needs is a new Fête de la Fédération, in which all the components of the nation could meet. But for the time being there is no organized political force able to free France from its European crust so that *nation* will naturally mean *generosity*, and the old lower-class milieus in France will be reconciled with French Muslims. This force, starting out from the zone of the egalitarian nuclear family, would gather together, in the name of an egalitarian doctrine, the educated young people who are falling into poverty, the lower-class milieus that have been relegated to the peripheries of our towns and cities, and French people of North African origin. Together, they would shove aside the historic MEZ bloc that unites executives, the elderly and zombie Catholics in their acceptance of inequality and their defence of privilege. But it is unlikely, even in the mid-term, that any such force will emerge.

The political system has gone haywire: it sees the left dominating in inegalitarian regions and the right in egalitarian zones. This dysfunction is going to last and even, for a few more years, get worse. The electoral body is continuing to grow old, which might lead to an even more fraught system. How can we hope for a crisis of 'conscience' to affect citizens whose median age is not just close to 50, in 2015, but is rising by 0.2 to 0.3 year per annum?[1]

Figure C.1 shows how fast this aging has been: nobody had foreseen it. Around 1950, a man aged 60 could expect to live for another 15 years, but in 2015 it is another 22 years; in 1950, a 60-year-old woman had another 18 years ahead of her, but in 2015 it is 27 years. François Héran, who was Director of the Institut national d'études démographiques, used a brilliant metaphor to suggest that the massive increase in the number of elderly could be analysed as an unforeseen and uncontrolled form of immigration.[2]

Charlie will grow old and his good conscience will become even more evident. Nostalgia for his childhood will gnaw at him more and more: he spent his youth in the heart of a white France where, in the absence of halal butchers but with fish in schools on Fridays, Church and Revolution coexisted.

Yes, things will probably get worse. Before they turn out all right?

---

[1] On the way age structures social life, see Hakim El Karoui, *La Lutte des âges. Comment les retraités ont pris le pouvoir* (Paris: Flammarion, 2013).
[2] François Héran, *Le Temps des immigrés* (Paris: Seuil/La République des Idées, 2007), pp. 87–89.

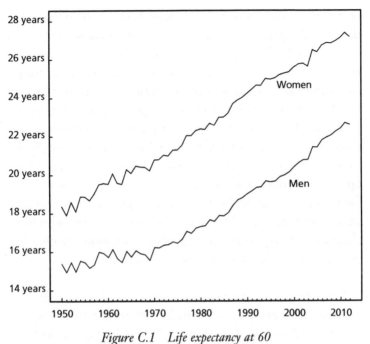

Figure C.1   Life expectancy at 60

The secret weapon of the republican revival

The culture of *la France centrale*, dominant in the heart of the Paris Basin and on the Mediterranean seafront, is struggling to mobilize the value of equality to obtain the best results. But it has not yet brought its secret weapon into battle.

In an excellent and very funny article on the diversity of the social sciences written over thirty years ago, the Norwegian Johan Galtung drew a comparison between the Anglo-American, Germanic, French and Japanese intellectual styles – he called them 'saxonic', 'teutonic', 'gallic' and 'nipponic'. He described English and American intellectuals as empirical in temper: imagining a multitude of modestly sized pyramids, they were not too downcast when one of their little constructions was shown to be invalid. He depicted the Japanese intellectual as a man (or woman) who could freewheel along, avoiding too close a commitment to any overdefinite model, concerned above all not to forget the complexity of the world. He drew a picture of German intellectuals as architects of one impressive single pyramid – but the Germans were prone to suffer a nervous breakdown if the falsity of their system was proved. Finally he came to French intellectuals, who, like the Germans, built up grand theories, which Galtung picturesquely described as hammocks strung between two poles, systems under tension never taken completely seriously by their authors, who were always in a hurry to escape any deep discussions by chatting over a nice lunch. Here is what Galtung says:

> It is my contention that the teutonic intellectual simply *believes* what he says, something his gallic counterpart would never really do ... I think the gallic intellectual would be more prone to consider his model as a metaphor, shedding some light on reality *but not to be taken too seriously*. (My emphasis)[1]

We might see this as just a Scandinavian twist on the hackneyed theme of French superficiality. But when we are talking about racism, the presence or absence of seriousness is a crucial sociological factor. For if anything can make racism really dangerous, it is seriousness. It is this that will lead a hundred white American families to move house when one or two black families move into their street, or will force the Germans, straining all their efforts in the First World

---

[1] 'Structure, Culture and Intellectual Styles: An Essay Comparing Saxonic, Teutonic, Gallic and Nipponic Approaches', *Social Science Information*, Sage, 20, 6, 1981, pp. 817–56 (p. 840).

War, to waste time checking that the Jews really are doing their military duty. It is the same seriousness that has just dragged Germany into the incredible 'debate' on child circumcision, concluding by bringing in a law to say that it was allowed for Muslims and Jews. The French are incapable of this kind of seriousness, which demands that people really respect the lines and borders defined by ideology. The attitude of *la France centrale*, imposed here, for its own good, on the whole periphery, evident in Charlie as in National Front voters and the kids in the suburbs, is nowhere more obvious than in the relations between the sexes. Concrete anthropology sees it as its task to convert the universal man of ideology into the universal woman of everyday life, the different concrete man into a different concrete man, much more difficult to reject than a concept, especially if she is very pretty. Hesitating between a beautiful exotic woman or an unalluring plump lass of home growth, the French universalist will usually make the right choice. And so will a French woman.[1] The absence of ideological gravity in the relations between the sexes is a basis on which we can build. It is in this way that France could remain itself, but above all it must not cultivate the ideology of blasphemy, exhort people to support the efforts in civic education, or make the defence of secularism a priority, and other such grandiloquent hogwash. France will perhaps get over this crisis because it is never, thank God, completely serious.

I have long had an absolute faith in my country's ability to assimilate immigrants of all origins – Jews, Asians, Muslims and Blacks. I have to admit that for some time I have started

---

[1] The priority given to the male perspective is not, here, the effect of any latent sexism: differentialism is particularly demonstrated by the refusal of men in the dominant group to take a wife from the dominated group. Thus, in the United States, the rate of mixed marriages is four or five times lower for black women than for black men.

to have my doubts. One day, perhaps, Paris will be one of
the planet's wonders, the city where representatives of all the
peoples of the world have melded together, a new Jerusalem
where the phenotypes separated by the dispersion of *Homo
sapiens* across the whole earth, for more than 100,000 years,
will have been mixed, brewed and recomposed into a human-
kind freed of all racial feeling. But it is certain that even if
France finally does manage to come back to herself, it will
be a much bumpier ride than I imagined twenty years ago.
And it is already clear that my generation will not see the
Promised Land.

Index

Page numbers in *italics* refer to maps, figures and tables